ESPN

THE NO-HOLDS-BARRED STORY OF POWER, EGO, MONEY, AND VISION THAT TRANSFORMED A CULTURE

ESPN

The No-Holds-Barred Story of Power, Ego, Money, and Vision that Transformed a Culture

Stuart Evey
with Irv Broughton

TRIUMPH
BOOKS
CHICAGO

Library of Congress Cataloging-in-Publication Data

Evey, Stuart, 1933–
    ESPN : the no-holds-barred story of power, ego, money, and vision that transformed a culture / Stuart Evey with Irv Broughton.
        p. cm.
    ISBN 1-57243-671-9
      1. ESPN (Television network)—History. 2. Television broadcasting of sports —History. I. Title.

GV742.3.E84 2004
384.55'5—dc22

                                                                    2004051723

This book is available in quantity at special discounts for your group or organization. For further information, contact:

Triumph Books
601 South LaSalle Street
Suite 500
Chicago, Illinois 60605
(312) 939-3330
Fax (312) 663-3557

Printed in U.S.A.
ISBN 1-57243-671-9
Design by Patricia Frey

All photos courtesy of Stuart Evey unless indicated otherwise.

To my wife, Mary, for her encouragement and support, and to
Christine and Susan, who shared their early life with ESPN.

Also,

to the employees of Getty Oil Company who supported this far-out
investment, and to the countless ESPN employees who made it happen.

CONTENTS

PREFACE

April 20, 2002, Lubbock, Texas. Spring in West Texas can be cold, but the reception from the members of the Lambda Tau chapter of Phi Gamma Delta and the alumni in the audience was warm and enthusiastic. Texas Tech University dominates the surrounding area both economically and psychologically. Sports, particularly football, command full attention, from pledges to parents. The spirit in the hall was high with camaraderie, school pride, and brotherhood as I came to the podium to address the gathering that night. The chapter was the envy of the fraternity system because a wealthy member had recently made it the most highly endowed chapter in the entire Greek system.

It was a hard decision as to what direction my remarks should take because I was not among those who had paid mega bucks to the brotherhood, but in the end, an old and deeply cherished relationship won out once again. That relationship was not to a woman, a lover, or a wife, but to a man whose trust and unfortunate, early death had shaped the direction of most of my entire career. This is part of what I said to them on a comfortable spring evening:

Yes, you are the envy of the fraternity, but with this comes an awesome responsibility. Brothers of Lambda Tau, many of you are nearing the end of your college years. As you embark into the next phase of your lives, I'm going to tell you a secret. It is my own secret of success. It is the reason I was involved with the launch of ESPN, the cable sports network. In fact, it was such a secret, I didn't know it myself until later in life: it's the secret of brotherhood.

I heard a saying when I was young. It goes something like this: "In order to build a strong relationship with a woman, you must first learn to build a strong relationship with a man." I learned my first lessons about brotherhood when I was a FIJI, back in the fifties. I didn't have a mama to take care of me anymore, so who took care of me? My brothers did, because I was one of them. And I learned that loyalty matters. I know that loyalty was not a popular word for a while because everyone was an individual who was going to pull himself up by the bootstraps, right into the Oval Office.

Well, I am here to tell you that it was the brotherhood of Phi Gamma Delta that is the foundation for what I am today. I was a working-class kid from Spokane, Washington. No one in my family had ever attended college. After spending a couple of years in the military, I went to the University of Washington in Seattle, where I had the good fortune to become a fraternity member.

I wondered if these young men, who were products of the boom-time nineties, could really comprehend what it was like a generation ago, and if they understood, would they even care? But I persisted with my story because the atmosphere in the room was focused intently upon me and seemed genuine.

When I graduated, I found a job with a small company in San Francisco, and that is where my lessons in brotherhood paid off. As a management trainee, my first job was moving furniture because the firm was relocating to Los Angeles. The assignment I was given was to arrange for the household furnishings of the executives to be shipped to their new homes in sunny Southern California. Most new employees would think that this was a demeaning, lackey task for a college graduate. But in my case, it turned out to be a big break, one that had a major impact on the rest of my entire professional life.

I could sense that there was some amusement in the audience, perhaps even a sense of skepticism.

In the process of getting the furniture moved out of a couple's home in suburban San Francisco, while I was chatting pleasantly with the lady of the house about details, the husband walked into the living room. That was my first meeting with George Getty, the son of J. Paul Getty, who was the richest man in the world at the time.

Now the young men were really interested. I continued.

George had just left military service himself, which gave us some frame of reference for a little conversation. I realized that there wasn't much a guy like me could do for a man like George, so instead of feeling inferior, I resolved to do everything I could for him. I did the best damn job of moving furniture that was humanly possible. And I like to think that George both saw and remembered that effort. My hunch paid off, and after the relocation, I was given a different job. The company made me a junior executive to assist the man in charge of the new office building, which meant I was a glorified super, but I made a point of being the very best building super anyone ever saw, and soon I was in charge of the entire building operation.

Management noticed me not because I was a big shot, but because there was no job too small for Stuart Evey. In 1962, after four years at the company, George Getty, my mentor, summoned me to his office. He told me that if I were to have a real career with the company, I needed to learn the oil business. He gave me an office next to his and said he would send information to me that would be helpful to my accelerated educational process. Living in the competitive and backbiting world as he did, George Getty was seeking someone he could trust to be loyal directly to him and no one else.

Soon, he assigned me all the organizations within the company which were not oil-related: corporate headquarters' human resources and public relations, real estate and agribusiness operations, and a resort hotel in Acapulco, Mexico. At the same time, I continued to be his executive assistant, managing his thoroughbred breeding and racing interests, and of course, his personal matters. Later in my career, lumber and plywood mills in the United States and Africa, as well as J. Paul Getty's personal estate in England, were added to these responsibilities.

What I did not share with this audience tonight was the fact that George had also trusted me with his substantial checking account while I was still just his executive assistant with the office next door to his own. Now came the harder part of the lesson in corporate ladder-climbing:

Not everything I did was pretty. In fact some of the tasks were downright ugly.

I did not share the specific facts with my mostly young audience that I had fired employees, procured drugs, and lied like a son-of-a-bitch if necessary and if my boss wanted it done for him.

I learned that there is a danger in loyalty, and that danger is blindness. You have to have a moral compass, and I regret to say that mine did not always point true north. However, I was driven to make sure everything I did was important to George Getty, and that is why I did it. I bought his homes and other assets in my name rather than in his, so people wouldn't take advantage of the Getty name. In taking care of his substantial thoroughbred racing interests, I knew that, in general, George Getty was not a happy man, despite the money. But when I called him to say that one of his horses won a race, the man was elated for a moment. And when he was happy, I was happy. For him, it had absolutely nothing to do with winning money because George was a member of one of the richest families in the world, but he got more joy and happiness from seeing his horse win a race than from anything else money could buy.

Maybe this is hard for people on the outside to understand, I thought, as I turned another page in my written speech, because at first, it was hard for me, too.

George Getty was actually the leader who made the modern Getty Oil Company a success, but his father was always quick to remind him that the old man was in majority control. I think George respected his father for his accomplishments as an oilman, but he never enjoyed the relationship between a father and son. Letters from his father were formally addressed to "Dear Mr. Getty," and no other way. George preceded his elderly father in death, and J. Paul Getty did not attend his funeral. However, I made every effort to be certain George Getty had a good relationship with me. He was like a brother, like a fraternity brother, and in some ways it cost me dearly. It likely led me down the road to overindulgences that might have killed me if I hadn't smartened up later in life. But in many ways, that relationship I had with George Getty was the defining relationship of my life.

ACKNOWLEDGMENTS

ESPN has been called "the most successful story in broadcast history." The network earned that assessment from its succession of ownership: Getty Oil Company staff at every level, ABC TV, Capital Cities Corporation, and the Disney Corporation.

All of them contributed blood, sweat, and tears—not to mention enormous talent and essential capital. *They took chances* to see it through. The unique talents of successive management leaders—Chet Simmons, Scotty Connal, Bill Grimes, Roger Werner, Steve Bornstein, and George Bodenheimer—made the phenomenal success of ESPN an almost taken-for-granted presence on the small screen.

I want to acknowledge the many employees of Getty Oil Company who gave so much time, effort, and dedication to bring this wild idea into the light of day. I am deeply grateful for their support. This is the first time I can publicly recognize the pioneering spirit of the employees of ESPN who were there when *SportsCenter* was beamed to the satellite from the broadcast center in Bristol, Connecticut, on September 7, 1979. They all had the desire to share the vision of reaching the ultimate goal: making ESPN the most popular sports television network. The formidable challenges they faced would make men and women of lesser stuff wilt. Their contributions in the beginning, followed by their successors, has made the enterprise a household word and changed the lives of generations of sports lovers forever.

ESPN

My personal thanks to those at ESPN who *never* let go of the dream: George Grande, Rosa Gatti, Dick Vitale, Barry Sacks, Lois Moreno, George Bodenheimer, and to all who have graciously shared their priceless memories. And to Bob McKinnon, Dave Henri, Don Rasmussen, Ed Hookstratten, Bob Creasy, Jack Leone, Herb Granath, and Mike Milardi, who all helped to jog my own memory to remind me of good times and bad, and the failures and successes. They have helped to make a media power become the stuff of legend.

And to Irv Broughton, and Mark Stimpfle, who worked under great pressure and eased the way in meeting those confounded deadlines. Together, they brought professionalism in recording and editing my past.

Lastly, to my wife and best friend, Mary, who encouraged me in this venture. It could not have been accomplished without the archives of history she has maintained over the years.

CHAPTER 1

INTIMATIONS OF MORTALITY

S tu, you better get over here quick. George is acting crazy, and I think he's trying to kill himself," the voice said over the phone. "He's out of control, Stu, but I think he'll listen to you . . . if he's still alive."

I'd been awakened from a sound sleep, and now I was standing balanced against my bed, gasping to claim some air.

"Please hurry, Stu, hurry . . . hurry." The voice was of desperation.

"I'll be there," I said. "I'm on my way." Then I turned to my wife, Shirley. "Something's wrong at the Getty's. Hurry and go with me." I grabbed for a shirt—any shirt—and as I ran out the door of my North Hollywood home, I felt my usually clear-eyed take on things begin to cloud. I usually wouldn't worry when an emergency call came in off hours because George Getty—or someone associated with Getty Oil Company—had a tendency to call at all hours, day or night. An emergency here, an emergency there, more company business, high-stakes company business. But this time, it was his wife, Jackie. I knew her well enough to know she didn't yield easily to panic and rarely betrayed anything more than a controlled formality, though she might be carried away now and then by whatever was the latest vogue among the wealthy.

This time, I recognized from her first breathless utterance that this was no hoax, and I shuddered at the vision of a doomsday scenario for this man George Getty, a deeply troubled man somehow always groping for the edge. I had glimpsed more than once his dark side.

The date was June 6, 1973, in Los Angeles, California. The call had come in the middle of the night.

Still, I clung to some notion it was a false alarm. Getty and his wife did fight a lot. And normal for George Getty was not normal for anyone else, but it sounded like this time he had found the edge and had gone over. Getty had suffered from periodic depression, often the result of binge drinking or excessive use of uppers and downers—or both. He didn't drink often, but when he did, he'd down 16 beers in a matter of an hour. I'd seen him do it. He popped heavy doses of diet pills at the slightest hint of weight gain. Sometimes all these conditions arrived simultaneously, and perhaps this was one of those times, I thought, as I raced to locate my keys. I had to collect my thoughts to formulate contingency plans and be ready for whatever circumstances I found when I arrived. I knew, deep down, that that level of preparedness was impossible.

But I told myself I could handle the situation. If Getty was alive, I would talk to him. It had to be all right. The powerful Getty family, led by George's father, J. Paul Getty, the richest man in the world, had depended on me to produce solutions, no matter what the conditions. So far I had never failed them—likely the dominant reason underlying my corporate success at Getty Oil. But what in hell awaited me tonight?

Like an old buddy, I was ready to curse Getty out for being put upon by his ruckus, and then to quickly forgive him the youthful folly. I might remind him that tomorrow was a horrific day for me. I had to negotiate a real estate project, a deal that would cost the company $2.5 million. I couldn't afford to be out all night just to get him to apologize and tell

2

him to be a good boy and keep the peace. Could it be so easy? No, not likely.

As I sped through the Los Angeles night, taking well-known side streets to avoid police and their radar, I thought of Getty, my friend, my colleague, my pillar of support. I thought of our years together. All the fun and craziness, all the earnestness, and, yes, the pain. A slight fog crept through the oaks and hung in the ravines like an enormous, fallen, white balloon. The fog forced me to slow down at times—more than I wanted.

I pulled up in front of the mansion, part of a gated community called Bel Aire, a prestigious residential area where the palatial estates and sweeping landscapes of the rich and famous stood. Recently, the community had seen the newly affluent move away into more glamorous surroundings, like Benedict Canyon above Beverly Hills or the yawning beaches of Malibu.

I jumped out, still buttoning my shirt. My wife, Shirley, followed me closely. Frantic, Jackie Getty flung open the door, and I entered the house feeling lost, as though I had never been there before. She told me she and Getty had planned to cook on the barbecue that night, but instead of a quiet dinner at home on the maid's night out, the evening had devolved into drinking and arguing. She said that Getty had become mad and mean, and then morose. He told her to "get out of his life or he would kill himself." She had taunted him, she admitted with a trace of guilt, saying that she "didn't think he had the nerve."

I scowled at her words, the brutal arrogance of them. And I could tell she knew the implications.

"Where is he now?" She pointed to their bedroom suite, situated upstairs at the back of the house, suspended there by a swirl of a staircase. "We've got to get into that room. Is he alive?"

"I think he's dead," she said. She inhaled deeply. "He could be."

3

My jaw dropped. We were both using words that came so naturally, "Oh yes, he might be dead." I glanced about, looking for a phone. I started to ask why she hadn't called the police. I caught myself because I knew.

I raced up the stairs with Getty's wife at my heels. She said, "He grabbed a knife from the barbecue and sliced himself across the stomach."

I turned away, put my ear to the door, knocked with the back of my hand. "George, it's Stu. George, please open the door. I need to talk to you." Brief pause—no answer. "We can work this out, George. George? Come on, old buddy. You're in there. I know you're in there. Don't do this." I turned to his wife and lowered my voice, "When did you last speak to him?"

"I haven't heard anything for a while."

I looked down at the carpet, saw the blood droplets tracking under the door, shut my eyes tight, opened them, and could feel my own body pulsing blood as if I were about to explode. I pounded on the door, pushing hard with my 165 pounds, trying to force it. "George! George, old buddy, you've got to open the door!"

He did not respond. I leaned close to the door and listened. I could hear him on the other side, snoring loudly. Maybe that was sleep, maybe just a drunken stupor.

"Oh no! Someone's outside," his wife said, apparently hearing a car pull up on the secluded driveway.

I leaned toward the upstairs window and saw the lights of a patrol car flashing in front of the house. "Let me handle this," I said, turning to her. Down the stairs I ran. I knew my role well. I was always in charge of chaos when it reared up in the Getty family business and in its family affairs. This would be no different, and I relied on that thought. Besides, Jackie couldn't—even in her urbane manner—explain away this one. She was weeping, her eyes red.

4

I longed to be home in my own bed, but as a kind of utility man on this team, I'd go in anytime, especially when the game got tough.

I hesitated for a moment at the door and worked to regain my composure. Then I opened the front door and stood face-to-face with two community patrol service officers. Apparently, they were required, at the time, to investigate everything when responding to unusual, late-night activity. A neighbor must have called in something.

"We've got a report about this place." The officer was short, bald-headed. Like a couple of wannabe detectives, he and his partner were taking stock of me.

"It's just a little family disagreement," I said.

"Family disagreement?" he repeated. The other guy—taller, leaner, circumspect—was quiet.

"You know how that can be, nothing unusual." I could feel the perspiration rising on my forehead, even though it was one of those rare cool Los Angeles nights.

"We got reports of yelling and screaming," the short officer said. I saw that Getty's wife was edging closer, and I beckoned behind my back for her to stop, which she did. By now, I was sweating and my face must have looked like I had emerged from my own bad, drunken evening.

"Probably the television," I said. "Must have jacked up the volume too much. You know, it's nothing. Just a husband and wife thing." The taller officer smiled knowingly.

"Well, I hope you understand we have to respond to any call," the short one said. The officers looked at each other, nodded agreement, and hustled down the front steps to their car in the driveway, sitting there with its still-flashing red, white, and blue lights. "Sorry if we bothered you," the tall one said, turning.

"No bother, officer," I said. They were within earshot when I acted querulous and chastised Jackie for coming out. We shut the door and returned to our post at the top of the stairs. I could still hear Getty snoring. I'd never had to deal with a drunk like this, but I'd heard of drug overdoses, some lethal. The victim would black out and then pass deeply, irretrievably, into a coma. No evidence was present that would indicate that possibility.

"We better call Dr. Smith." We went to the kitchen, referred to the posted list of emergency numbers, and dialed the doctor's number. "Stay here and listen," I instructed her.

The phone rang, and a drowsy voice cut into the silence. "Dr. Smith? This is Stu Evey calling from the Getty house. We've got an emergency situation with George. Can you come over?"

"What is it?" he said.

"He's alive, but he's bleeding from what appears to be a self-inflicted wound."

The doctor seemed to snap to. "I'll get there as soon as I can."

Dr. Kendrick Smith was a partner in the medical clinic Getty Oil retained for employees. He had been Getty's personal doctor for years. While we waited desperately for him to arrive, I tried to figure out how I could climb up the walls and break in through a window. It didn't look possible, and when Dr. Smith arrived, I was confident that together we could break down the bedroom door.

When the doctor finally arrived, we dispensed with any greetings and went to the bedroom. "Shall we give it a try?" Dr. Smith asked. We drove our bodies against the door, and finally, on the third try, the two of us were able to break it down. A pathetic sight greeted our success: Getty, as pale as his white boxer shorts, was lying on the floor, blood dripping down his stomach and onto the shorts. Then I saw the knife beside him. It, too, was stained with blood. He was still snoring loudly. How could he have survived that long? It reminded me of the character Neff in *Double Indemnity*, who bleeds to death over several hours while he dictates into a recorder his confession of murder.

The doctor stopped the bleeding. Getty shifted several times, and his breathing, once reason for hope, now portended the end of a man who would have the last laugh in an ongoing dispute with life—*probatum est*.

"Well, Jackie said he'd been drinking heavily—at least two bottles of wine and several beers. With that much, I would guess he's beyond drunk. Should we take him to UCLA?" I asked.

The doctor was surprisingly sanguine. "I don't know if we need to do that, particularly if you want to avoid publicity." The UCLA Medical Center was not far from Beverly Hills and West Los Angeles, and it was the chosen hospital for celebrities from those areas. As a result, the press had ready access to the personalities, especially those arriving by ambulance. Dr. Smith was affiliated with the Queen of Angels Hospital in central Los Angeles, and suggested we take him there, where we could take control of the admittance procedure. But I knew the call was mine: it was my corporate job to make this decision. I was worried about the very unfavorable publicity for Getty—my boss, my friend—the Getty family, his father, and the company. I could just imagine the lurid stories in the tabloids, the insidious gossip, the inquiry by the company board of directors. I had to figure a way to feed the press a story, anything that took the bitter focus away.

We called an ambulance, but before it arrived, I took the knife, wrapped it in a towel, and gave it to my wife, Shirley, to clean. I told her to then return it to its proper place in the kitchen drawer and to ditch the towel. When the ambulance arrived, a couple of EMTs in white jackets got out and loaded Getty's barely living body in back. I rode along to Queen of Angels Hospital. The streets were all but deserted.

Once we reached the admittance area, I still had to try to control things. Getty couldn't be George Getty. At my insistence, Dr. Smith admitted him under an assumed name. I don't know why, but the name of my friend, Heisman Trophy winner Glenn Davis, came to mind. No questions were asked, and I gave Getty's home address as that of my own in North Hollywood. The plan developing in my mind was that when he awoke and was strong enough to talk, I would encourage him to leave town immediately to spend some time in a remote location with an excuse that he had an acute viral infection or some plausible illness, the treatment of which demanded uninterrupted rest. We could then develop the next strategy to deal with the matters at hand, both at home and at the company. I hated that I seemed worried more about others' reaction to the situation than with Getty himself. But I was trained that way. I got over it—fast.

"Have you arranged for a private room?" I asked Dr. Smith.

"Yes," he responded. His mouth was a straight line. Over the rim of his reading glasses, he looked mildly put out. In the private room I observed that a heart monitor, IV, and oxygen were hooked up to Getty. Thinking he was stabilized for the moment, I went to sleep on the floor next to the bed. There was no couch and the floor was certainly more comfortable than a metal chair. It was now close to two in the morning. I don't know how I slept, but I was drained and fell to sleep in probably just a few moments.

The next thing I remembered was being jolted out of a deep sleep by a commotion in the room. Nurses, doctors, and attendants were walking over me and surrounding him. They told me he had fallen into a coma. It was shocking news. A few minutes later, a doctor informed me that Getty's heart had stopped for a lengthy period, and there could be damage to his brain. He was very guarded about the chance of recovery.

I had no choice but to call his father, J. Paul Getty, in England. In my confused state, I still could calculate that the early morning time in Los Angeles meant late afternoon in England. It would be easy for me to tell

him his son had suffered a minor stroke, that it was still too early to determine the degree of seriousness. I decided I had to do just that. It's like
having too much bad news to give all at once; the human tendency is to
soft-pedal; it was my tendency. This white lie was certainly not the first I
had told, nor would it be the last.

My first call to Mr. Getty went to Sutton Place, his home near Guildford, England, about 35 miles outside London. I was informed by his secretary, Barbara Wallace, that Mr. Getty could be reached at the home of
longtime friend, the Duchess of Argyll, in London. I was given the
number, and I placed the call. The duchess herself answered. I introduced
myself and asked if I might speak to Mr. Getty on a matter of great importance. J. Paul Getty took the phone, and I began: "Mr. Getty, I've got bad
news about George. He suffered a stroke early this morning at his home
and was taken to the hospital. It is too early to determine the extent of his
illness, but I wanted you to be the first to know."

From the tone of his voice, it was obvious he was shocked and dis-
mayed at the news, and he asked that I keep him informed of further
developments—whatever the time of day. He knew I would. I then mentioned that he might want to consider an acting replacement at the
company for George, until such time as he recovered and returned. "Who
should that be?" he responded.

That comment really took me aback. Here I was, being asked by J.
Paul Getty to recommend an acting executive to replace the executive vice
president and chief operating officer of the seventh largest oil company in
the world. This decision could have far-reaching implications, knowing
what the doctor had just told me a few minutes before, that Getty's recovery was questionable.

I recalled a letter Getty had written to his father listing executives he
thought could be considered for senior positions in the future. One was

9

Sidney R. Petersen, then the chief financial officer. The younger Getty did not consider himself as strictly an oil man, but rather a businessman, interested in widely ranging subjects, and recognized that many of the oil companies were now choosing their leaders from the fields of legal, financial, and economic backgrounds. He had an affinity for the same in Getty Oil, and often commented that the days of "good ol' boys from the oil patch" was no longer a prerequisite to lead an oil company. Sid Petersen was the type Getty would recommend. Mr. Getty recalled the letter and George's thoughts on the subject, and asked that I issue a corporate press release that Sidney R. Petersen would be acting executive vice president and chief operating officer until George Getty could step back into that position. Needless to say, when that decision was made public, it raised the ire of the company's top oil executives and some of the members of the company's board of directors.

After concluding the call to Mr. Getty, I phoned Getty's mother, Jeanette Jones, and told her exactly what had transpired. I suggested she come to the hospital to be there when more news was given. I also phoned Jackie, who said she would come also.

When Mrs. Jones arrived, I got her together with Dr. Smith to give her a full explanation of Getty's condition. When his wife arrived, she ran to me and said she needed to talk. We went into a vacant waiting room, where she informed me that when Dr. Smith and I were in the bedroom with Getty, she looked in the bathroom and noticed two empty pill bottles, which she hid in the clothes hamper. She didn't know if he had taken any of the barbiturates, and she didn't want anyone else to know that she knew of those bottles, especially if his condition were revealed to be anything more than severe drunkenness.

"Good God, Jackie, do you know the situation with George now? He's in a coma, caused by who knows what, but if you had mentioned it, we could have been safe and taken George across the street to UCLA. We could have had his stomach pumped." I informed Dr. Smith of this new information. We decided that such a disclosure would serve no purpose now.

I went to the office, arriving about 6:30 A.M., dressed in the same clothes I had worn since being called to the Getty house. I sat quietly in my office drinking coffee and contemplating the next course of action. When the office secretaries arrived, I told them Getty would not be in and that he had decided to go down to his beach house for the day. Apparently, my being unshaven, disheveled, and dressed casually were no cause for them to probe deeper. They probably thought I'd forgotten it was a work day.

Soon Sid Petersen arrived. We went in to George Getty's office, where I proceeded to give him the whole story, including the prognosis for Getty at the time, and I recounted my discussion with J. Paul Getty. Petersen's reaction was one of disbelief, shock, and, likely, apprehension for both the fallout and his assignment to make the announcement.

Later that same morning, George Getty died. He never regained consciousness. That afternoon, Jackie Getty accepted friends and business associates at the house to pay their respects. Laura Mako, a family friend, and my wife, Shirley, prepared snacks. Shirley often said she'd never forget the eerie feeling she got when she watched Mako using the knife to chop lettuce, the same knife she had cleaned of blood the night before.

All the lies I had told in trying to protect Getty from a family feud and celebrity scandal were suddenly unraveling in front of me. While they were all well intended, and all motivated by the question, "What would George want me to do?" they were nevertheless misguided. I had agreed to conceal evidence: to cover up his wife's pill bottle disclosure, to clean the knife and have it put away, and to admit him to a hospital under a false identity. All my actions were justified in my own mind because the man had been like a brother to me—not just my boss, not just my mentor, and not just because

11

he was the man who had taken me into his confidence—and as a result, he had made my own career possible. I could not construe my actions as a cover-up. Rather, they stemmed from a conviction that he would have wanted it exactly the way I managed to recreate it for public consumption. The way I saw my behavior, I had done nothing wrong. Everything I did was to protect the image of the one person in the world to whom I owed everything in my adult life. Nothing was premeditated. I made tough decisions, and I often had to make them spontaneously—the result of years of careful training, years of learning what is now called "spin," and which is really nothing more than putting a positive face on screw-ups.

No matter, George Getty was dead. Whether his suicide was intentional or accidental no longer made a difference. My boss, mentor, brother, friend was gone. Like a man sleepwalking, I attended to the details of the funeral, the press releases, the mourners, and the family.

The loss had a profound impact on me. While I remained in the same job—running the nonoil operations that were, individually, the size of many important corporations—I could no longer summon the motivation that had always driven me in the past. With his untimely death, I had not only lost George Getty, I seemed to have lost my reason to excel. Getty was gone, and I had no one to please anymore. For five long years, I simply went through the motions of showing up for work and being alive. I drank. I disappointed myself. I know now it would have disappointed Getty, who was, as I have said, like a brother or a father to me.

Then, quite out of the blue, a stranger appeared with the crazy idea for a cable sports television network—ESP-TV. I would have to force myself to think I could do anything I wanted to once again, and I would have to accomplish whatever I could muster, without Getty—without my friend, George.

CHAPTER 2

Early Years
and Nascent Notions

I grew up small. I was just 4'11" when I graduated from high school. But I ended up markedly taller: I grew about nine inches during my first year of college. I grew up in a family of modest means—my father worked for the Great Northern Railroad. But I quickly grew rich and, by most measures, successful, if not mostly forgotten. This is the story of that growth and the remarkable spurt it underwent, just as I did, that freshman year, toward my role in founding a telecommunications giant and the astounding, mercurial success that followed. It's my story of ESPN.

The chronicle really begins in Havre, Montana. That's where I was born in 1933.

Outside of Havre, about 15 miles from where I grew up, sits a squat range known as the Bear's Paw Mountains, a nub of peaks that look more like a sad gathering of wayward buffalo that might have fallen from one of the cliffs. The locals might say, with some contempt, that the Bear's Paws seemed more like hills than mountains, more "like mountains in the East." That must have been the first disparagement I heard about the East. It certainly wasn't the last.

Anyone trying to survey the land from the Bear Paw Mountains would note a dramatically contrasting plainscape: flatland, expanses, and lots of dryland wheat farming—most call it ranching around these parts—the area's main industry. Winter rolls in quickly and sticks around much too long, reminding those of us on the khaki-pale earth that nature is boss. What William Faulkner wrote in *As I Lay Dying* seems written for this place: "Everything, weather, all, hangs on too long."

I was only six when my family left Havre to move to Whitefish, Montana. There was no struggle in Father's mind, I don't believe, about the decision. You followed your job, which was with the Great Northern Railroad and, as they say, the rails do lead in every direction. Dad came home one day and produced a transfer notice that ultimately sent us all off to Spokane, where we looked out on vacant, grassy fields dotted with a few trees.

I was 12 and, like most kids, anxious to prove myself in sports. Unfortunately, I was woefully small for my age. I stood just 4'7" and weighed probably no more than 75 pounds. We kids would build forts and romp like little Huck Finns, always wondering and delighted with what the world had in store for the day. Later, of course, I would have plans for just about every day of my life. During my first years in Spokane, I pitched for a Junior American Legion baseball team and managed to pitch a no-hit, no-run little gem of a game.

While I longed for sports, they were mostly an excuse to get together with my pals. I never had the win-at-all-costs mentality, not in sports, although I was compelled to develop such a mindset later in business to succeed. I always considered it fun to win, but not at all costs. Now and then, I'll recall that time and think that had I played, I would not have come to see the value in supporting others quite so keenly. I always reveled in the athletic success of my many athlete friends. Appreciating others and cheering them on occurs in business too, but not always as often as it should. Why not be happy for others' accomplishments? They might even be happy for yours.

We later moved to a nice brick home overlooking the railroad tracks, as if a reminder of Dad's success—or failure. I discovered the sport of pool and acquired some expertise at a large mom-and-pop pool hall. Lights hung, pendulous and close, over the green-gray tabletops, illuminating the players against a dark background tinted garishly with tobacco smoke in a spectral light that suggested a modest spotlight on celebrity. The waiting players, the watchers, hung back in the darkness. I gained a lot of confidence from my skill at pool and took a fine pleasure in experiencing my diminutive stature as no limiting factor in sporting competition. We played a game called "live pool." Each player bought a ball to play as his own, each ball, of course, bearing its own number. The game required shooting at any ball lower in number. Send the lower-numbered ball into the hole, and victory was assured.

Though my parents knew nothing of it, we gambled on the games. Everybody would wrangle a loan of, or otherwise muster, 15¢ and drop it, ringing, into a large iron pot. The winner claimed the proceeds, which, in those days, could be as much as $3 or $4, not an insignificant sum, and one that enabled a splurge on the weekend, including all the Cokes one could drink and, for the reckless, all the cigarettes one could smoke.

I spent considerable time at the many lakes around Spokane, especially Diamond and Loon, the summer before my freshman year at college. Then I was off to Washington State University. I lasted there one term before I transferred to the University of Washington, where I joined several friends who introduced me to the life of houseboys at the Alpha Gamma Delta sorority. We felt like our time had come; we lived in the basement, and the sweet voices of girls singing or gossiping charmed the daylights out of us as if they were angels from above.

Then I decided to take some business courses at Seattle University. I liked the University of Washington and had developed a lifetime of friendships there, but Seattle University had something even the bigger university did not. It featured a pair of basketball players who were soon vaulted to heights unknown to most shorter players. They were the O'Brien twins, Eddie and Johnny, each only 5'9". By taking courses at Seattle University, I got an athletic card that would let me in to all the school's basketball games. Time after time, I watched those wily little Irishmen dash through small openings in the defense for layups or pull up suddenly for jump shots. They would release the ball so quickly that it almost seemed as if they could not stand the heat in their hot shooting hands. I attended the games and felt a near-obsession with them, as if little guys could—and would—overcome.

My sporting life, my life as a follower, really, had its price. I had begun to perform poorly in college, and the tolerance for my trifling began to wear thin. I was on academic probation for a while, and my mother saw this as another mark of failure. I knew I wasn't applying myself, and when I tried to turn a failing relationship around, my girlfriend turned her back on me.

Disheartened and upset, I volunteered for the draft and, in 1954, entered the U.S. Army. I had taken some reserve training in college, and the transition felt less steep than it might have otherwise. Or maybe life was beginning to sober me. Anyway, the military sent me to Ft. Ord in California for boot camp and training.

One day an officer appeared with a narrow band of fabric in his hand. As he opened his hand wider, I could see he held a stripe, which he handed to me—a reward for my reserve training. Promptly, the stripe found a proud place on my arm. More and more, I felt like a general, although I only moved up to platoon leader with this new recognition. That award taught me something about the value of preparation, how we build for the future, sometimes without even knowing as much.

One day I heard some zealous footsteps bearing down on me. I turned to see a sergeant. "Private Evey, you are to go to the gymnasium at 1400 hours."

I snapped a salute. "Yes, sir!" I hollered.

When the time came, I apprehensively stepped inside of the carrier-sized gym, and before me, hundreds of recruits lined up in precision. The commanding general of the base beckoned to me and, sheepishly, I strode toward him. I saluted him. He marched me out in front of the troops. I remember he was tall and had close-set eyes that were bright as candles. There in the almighty shade of him, nervous and sweating, I shook, and he positioned himself to speak. I wondered what I had done wrong. I did have the one stripe, but didn't think I'd accomplished much since. I ran slower than most of the others in exercise. I was certainly no standout in softball games, or anything else that I could recall. But I was on time, and I did get to know the drill sergeant. Then, the general spoke: "Be an outstanding person like this gentleman," he told the assembled soldiers. I must have touched my stripe like a four-leaf clover.

I owe the military for the serious take on life that they offered me, and for several things I took away with me from that experience. I came to realize that, in the activities, hidden or noticed, in life, there are shepherds and there are sheep. That's the world, a grand dichotomy, and one part is not better than the other; both need and depend upon each other. Meeting that simple idea head-on, an approach gathered from my army experience, gave me some tremendous insight in judging people and reacting and in decision-making for the real world. I have been reminded time after time of this truism in my business pursuits.

When we had begun to glimpse the end of boot camp, I found that my new status had some positive impacts on my choices for future duty.

My superiors, who had another stripe or two, told me that I could stay there with them and be a drill instructor, take a duty shift at the Tomb of the Unknown Soldier, or attend the U.S. Embassy as a member of the honor guard in Berlin, Germany. Already I felt I had gained confidence and would not choose the easiest option, though none of them seemed difficult. But I chose the honor guard, and on a chilly November day, I boarded the USS *Stewart*.

We landed in Bremerhaven in the northern part of Germany near Hamburg, and soon the military had loaded us, to eerie displeasure, on blacked-out trains. We felt almost like tourists with blinders on, and only a few lines of light pierced the walls as we slowly made our way down the tracks through the Russian-occupied sector of the great divided city, once a haven for high culture in Europe.

The honor guard, in the new embassy uniforms, cut a fine figure with chrome helmets, patent leather boots, and silver on the guns. In any light, we seemed to shine. Furthermore, our jeep bore still more chrome. An observer might have thought us not electric, but metallic.

In Berlin, we stood guard in front of the embassy, serving under General Lucius Clay, an affable man with a fading hairline and a relative of the famous Kentucky senator, Henry Clay. Appointed military governor of Germany, General Clay, who oversaw the troubled times after the war when food and survival were sometimes in question, was revered by the German people. In fact, after his death, the citizens of Berlin, then with a population of 2.5 million, offered a plaque with the words: "We thank the defender of our freedom."

The honor guards role was largely ceremonial. We presided over celebrity visits, and when the film *The Conqueror* premiered there, we drew our circles around Susan Hayward and John Wayne.

I had matured, and after a two-year term, I returned to the United States and to the University of Washington. This time, my aim was as clear as a chrome gun's barrel. I applied myself; I planned to graduate this time, although I could not desert my beloved sports or my studies. I ended up, once again, watching Seattle University basketball games and found a new hero.

Now the basketball player in Seattle drawing raves was a young man, a transfer from the College of Idaho, by the name of Elgin Baylor. Without regard for traditions of race or even those of basketball, Baylor set the court on fire and, again, I was there. It was almost like he was playing in a game of H-O-R-S-E, where one player has to make the shot his opponent makes. Here, Baylor was taking the same kind of unusual, challenging shots, but the difference, of course, was that he was doing it in an actual game. The shots were neither for show nor to showcase their degree of difficulty. They were done, as needed, to score. And score he did. I sat mesmerized many, many nights as I watched swarming defenses try everything to stop or slow him, as he whirled, spun, posted, dipped, climbed, and faded away. Baylor would get 41 points one night, 45 another.

During his career at Seattle University, Baylor averaged more than 29 points a game; he averaged more than 27 per game during his pro career before his knees tired of the punishment from takeoffs and landings. When he left Seattle University for the pros, I felt like an insider, like someone in on the ground floor of a franchise. I followed him closely and relished his professional accomplishments, including the amazing 71-point game against the New York Knicks. A little more than a decade ago, the great pro Jerry West told *Hoops* magazine, "I haven't seen many that compare with him." As the human species seems to get taller, faster, and stronger, Baylor still stands out as an American original—one of the greatest to play the game.

For some, a part of life dwells for a spell on the notion of repeated failure, which begins to sink in. Not for me. I began to plan my sports watching so that I could still perform in my studies. I knew I was capable.

After all, I had gotten so far ahead in school at John R. Rogers High School that the school had me sit out a term and then join my classmates to graduate on time with them.

My parents were still alive when I had returned to college after my military service. But the last years of one's life with a beloved parent often pass bittersweetly. I try not to remember the last five years with my mother, whom the family had to place in different "old folks" homes. This seldom worked out, for Mother was a different person at that stage in her life. She was like a little princess, irascible, complicated, and argumentative. At times, after a period of a few weeks of calm, I would get the dreaded call that she was acting up. She needed to be moved to another place. All during that time, she had refused to stop smoking, and for some reason, this bothered me enormously. In the narrowing of alternatives, I would reminisce to myself about the trip my parents and I had taken to J. Paul Getty's estate, Sutton Place, in England. We made that trip in 1977, after I had been working for the Gettys for some time. We arrived on Mother's birthday and celebrated it there. Mother was excited—this was status, the heights. The staff prepared a cake and delivered a card with the signature of nearly everyone in the household. One could almost hear the sound of trumpets rippling across the open lawns and manicured fields of the vast estate.

With my father, the last years meant a summing up, if not a reckoning, of our relationship. In 1974, I decided to rent the family a motor home and travel with them across Europe. I found a modest-sized Tioga in London and, joined by my wife, Shirley, and two children, Christine and Susan, in-laws Ray and Beatrice Kinne, and my parents Clare and Evelyn Evey, we departed Dover for continental Europe on a ferry. To everyone's delight, we traveled across the English Channel on our way to tour France and Germany.

As our entourage passed through the French countryside, we must have stood out as modern-day hillbillies—we nearly overflowed the vehicle with the nine of us angled everywhere, looking wide-eyed out the windows. People all along the road laughed as we appeared, as if they were glimpsing an amusing carnival act. French roads, winding and circuitous, difficult enough to negotiate even in a small vehicle, can easily tire a motorist.

At one point outside of Paris I realized we were lost. I pulled over to the side of the road and, finally frustrated with shuffling through the maps, I turned to Dad, who was sitting like a general beside me in the front seat. "Go find out where Rheims is, would you?" Dad slid out the door and headed for a convenience store, the French equivalent of a 7-Eleven.

When I looked over at the store a few minutes later, he was still talking. There he stood next to an elderly Frenchman sporting a mustache and beret. Dad was nodding, and the Frenchman was gesturing. After a few more minutes, the exchange concluded with a flourish of waving, accented by cordial smiles. Finally, as he seemed to really understand, Dad nodded once and beelined back to the motor home, where I took on a fresh optimism.

I just knew that we were as good as there or, at least, I figured Dad had found out the right road. When he finally stepped up and into the front seat, happy and beaming, I was confident we were on our way—the right way to Rheims, to the heart of the French wine country. "Where are we going? Which way?" I asked.

"I don't know," Dad said, pausing. "He doesn't speak English."

I subdued my rising irritation. By then, my understanding of my father's character and decision-making had changed and matured enough for me to respect him for who he was, and that understanding brought me no small measure of peace.

The knowledge that a father not only loves you—which I feel he always did—but also is proud, genuinely proud, of you is an assurance I think my spirit needed. I think any son needs such love. And when someone is proud, the world knows it, and that means something, however small that world may be. He would visit his longtime friends Joe and Tony Zappone every time he had news to report on my activities that were taking me all over the world and country. They were local sports enthusiasts and often promoted boxing events, both amateur and professional. My father was always proud of my accomplishments at Getty Oil Company before ESPN, and would take great pride in sharing information about me with his friends.

Many times, Mary and I would show up, flying from California on holidays, but mostly for whatever occasion we could justify, to find my father framed there in the doorway, sitting patiently cross-legged, exuding his brand of fatherly pride. On one memorable visit, I noticed more in his posturing than his usual energetic look, a look difficult to describe. It was that of someone who was in his place completely, body and soul. I remember pausing as I gazed at him, as I recalled suddenly that soul of his.

Most people cannot hide pride with any real grace, and it was obvious that Dad was no different in his buoyant regard for my success. He took an invigorated pleasure, in fact, in introducing me to people. I never knew he had so many friends, and he'd corner Joe or Harry or Paul or George or Lily or Martha, calling out introductions around the outside of a bridge table or down the street. It didn't embarrass me really, but the introductions, hurled louder than one would an insult and occasionally across the din of a post office, could make any young man wish he could reach for the nearest doorknob and start running.

Not that Dad and I hadn't had rifts, or perhaps tensions, in our relationship. Dad had been a quiet drinker for years—an almost secret drinker—but his drinking colored our lives. It's not that he straggled home every day, worn to the heels with drink, but rather that his addiction had a negative effect on Mother. Mother, bless her soul, was no saint. She was a social climber, who had grown increasingly frustrated over the years by Father's drinking and its effects. When I grew older and gained insight, I felt that Dad's problem stemmed from the fact that he could not, or was not willing to pay the price of ambition. And that responsibility does exact its price. Mother watched the rise of his peers as they shuffled up through the company ranks; she watched and she stewed. Though Father did rise some in the company's hierarchy, she nonetheless blamed him, and the tension, at times, registered on her face.

Sometime in the early days of ESPN, I received a call from Dad. "They're having a big boxing thing in Spokane," Dad said. "Do you think ESPN can do it?" I was flabbergasted. My dad, the man from the railroad business, had an idea for programming.

"I don't think so, Dad," I said. We had an insatiable appetite for programming in those days and at least considered most everything, but I wasn't altogether sure we were that hungry. Still, I reflected on the notion. It was the Western Olympic Trials, which sounded interesting, although President Jimmy Carter had decided that the United States would boycott that year's Olympics, a fact that took off some of the luster and a hell of a lot of the draw for most involved. For the bigger names in boxing, the Olympics were no longer the show, and because of that, some fighters decided early to turn professional. Still, Spokane was a good sports town, and its many sports fans would no doubt support the fights. I thought I'd see if I could please Dad, and maybe we could do it with just one camera. "Let me call you back," I said.

I had really made the decision while we spoke, but I needed to call ESPN President Chet Simmons for a consultation and his approval.

Simmons gave me the go-ahead, and ESPN wound up broadcasting the two final matches on May 31, 1980, at the Spokane Coliseum. ESPN contracted with a local production company, and we brought Sean O'Grady from Los Angeles to give a blow-by-blow description of the fight.

Surprisingly, the event turned out well. Dad had accidentally stumbled onto something. Several of the fighters from Los Angeles, including Jimmy Ellis, who was later to become the world champion, had actually sparred with Muhammad Ali. In the finals, the crowd cheered its own Mike DeLaPena of Spokane, who was later bested by Sammy Fuentes in a split decision. And another, Alex DeLucia of Portland, won a unanimous decision over Tony Tucker, who was ranked number one in his bracket among the world's amateurs at the time. DeLucia was victorious despite Tucker's frequent clinching, done to hold off the onslaught—an unfavorable, although acceptable, tactic among aficionados.

That night, I had worried about Dad's ability to coordinate things, but he made it to the airport to pick up O'Grady and didn't get lost. But he *did* get lost another time, while transporting Jim Simpson, ESPN's outstanding sportscaster, and Bud Wilkinson, the great University of Oklahoma football coach, who had come out to broadcast a Washington State football game. They were late to a party, which prompted Simpson to quip, "It caused me to miss the first three drinks."

Joe Zappone, whose father, Jack, promoted the Western Olympic Trials, said to me once about Dad, "He was our ESPN man. We even introduced him at ringside!" Several weeks later, as a kind of joke, I had business cards printed up for him that read: "Clare Evey, Northwest ESPN Rep." The smile on my father's aging but still handsome face is an image forever etched in my mind.

I came to love the easy, open Dad of those years, and I was, at last, able to share completely with him, to connect with him more certainly than I had previously believed possible. More than that, I cherished having him see me succeed in a tough world and in a field of my choosing, noting that he had no hand in directing me. I staked my claim separately and, therefore, found my own sense of pride.

Some time after I had risen to vice president of diversified operations at Getty Oil and been made chairman of ESPN, I drove down to Van Nuys Airport and signed for a Westwind airplane, one of seven passenger airplanes owned by the Getty company. With two company pilots and several associates, we flew to Spokane, where I picked up my dad. We flew him to the Final Four in Albuquerque, New Mexico, where North Carolina State University capitalized on a last-minute play by Derek Whittenberg to gain a 54–52 victory and the national championship. University of Houston coach Guy Lewis and Clyde "the Glide" Drexler, among others, went sadly home, but I still remember North Carolina's coach, Jim Valvano, racing through the gym.

On the plane to Albuquerque, I closed my eyes and felt I'd dreamed it all. Despite the demands of the corporate life, some very precious time had allowed me to be with my father in the fullest and maybe the grandest of times.

At the Final Four, sports luminaries, glitterati, and personalities filled the hospitality suite. Don Ohlmeyer, then of NBC Sports, was there. So was Bryant Gumbel, along with many others, including some memorable, colorful coaches. Dick Vitale attended, and he and my dad joked and carried on a conversation for some time off in the corner of the room. Soon other people ventured near, spun off quick yarns, and treated my father as if he had just joined a distinguished fraternity. I'd never seen him happier than he was that night—the new recruit, spending his time observing his new school and damned glad to be there.

My father took from the experience a deep satisfaction, not because he held himself up as a sports aficionado (Dad had played no organized sports during his life; he preferred the occasional fishing trip to the north fork of the Clark Fork River and Whitefish Lake in Montana), but because he was more than a remote spectator. He was in a world he thought he'd never be a part of, hobnobbing with sports heroes he'd only read about or seen on TV. Together, Dad and I seemed a long way from Havre, Montana.

Dad died in 1994, and I took joy in the fact that when I looked around at the large crowd at his funeral I saw so many of my friends and his. No one ever gets enough time with a loved one. Drinking loomed large with him, and I felt sorry for the time I missed as a result. Indeed, drinking loomed large for me later, and I think I understand him more for that sad experience. I think now of my father, and how his death has come back to me vividly many, many times. And on this or that day, my mind will flash back to this story or that, especially back to the time I had planned to leave the state and he met me for an unhurried good-bye.

It was late spring, and I had graduated from the School of Business at the University of Washington. I can remember the white and purple crocuses forming little hoods under the blossoming oriental cherry trees. Spring is a time of beauty-unashamed in Seattle. The cherry blossoms, when they leave, usually leave all at once, flushed by a good wind—a wave of colored pixels in the air as they skitter away. What I felt was the Japanese idea of transience and ethereal ephemera. That is why the Japanese embrace the cherry blossoms and their symbolism. I needed to leave.

Dad and I got together over dinner at the Rainier Club in Seattle. I told him about my plan to drive down to California and get some work. On the way home after a nice dinner, I said something about how it would make it easier for me if he could give me some money. He turned around in the front seat of the car and wedged himself tightly against the door.

"Son, you've been eating steak for a long time." I feared where this was leading. "Maybe it's time to eat some hamburger," he said.

"I can't have any money?" I mumbled and slurred.

"No, I think not." He checked his watch. "You best get on the road. You've got a 30-hour drive."

It sounded like a lesson, but one that I thought he was trying to teach a little late. We embraced for a few moments. He touched me once on the face, and I climbed into my car.

I felt free, and like young people everywhere, I buffered the more negative thoughts with confidence that I could, and would, set the world on fire. Breaking the perimeters of home doesn't guarantee freedom. I wasn't truly free, not yet.

CHAPTER 3

WORK STYLES OF THE RICH AND FAMOUS

At Getty Oil, serving as vice president of the diversified operations division, I worked closely with the rich and famous George Getty. Getty seemed to need someone he could count on, and I was that person. He wasn't altogether comfortable with some members of the company, but he seemed to be so with me. I was his right-hand man, but the status posed a Herculean challenge: I was running a major multimillion-dollar operation, a wide-ranging sphere of business comprising real estate, agricultural and forest products, and public relations and human resources. At the same time, I was executive assistant to the executive vice president and chief executive officer, George F. Getty II, eldest son of J. Paul Getty, who was, at the time, the richest private citizen in the world.

George Getty was a detail man, a man of large and small concerns. Dealing with and resolving many of the small concerns was certainly not listed in my job description, but I was charged with a virtual regimen of chores, both Getty Oil's and Getty's. Most executives would have found these little responsibilities annoying, and others would have been overwhelmed with the downright impossible tasks; the burden certainly would have turned the average person away to seek employment elsewhere, where rank had privilege.

Somehow, though, I didn't mind. I figured I could learn—possibly in small ways—from Getty. To accomplish this, I'd meet him in his office nearly every day, shortly after his arrival, and he'd briefly review and assign all that he needed me to do at that time. Early on, I was supplied with a box of small, 3x2 inch notepads. Such a notepad had to accompany me at all times, and furthermore, I had to use it. If I didn't have a notepad, Getty would stare me down like I had forgotten my socks. It was as though my private behavior had gone public, and I'd glance about to see if someone else was watching. Sometimes, I was made to feel less than adequate. I'd hastily pull out the notepad, and he'd do likewise. Then we could begin to scratch out a list—one item to a page—of the everyday work, often of portentous and ponderous proportions, he had elected to assign to me for the day. You might find amusing the following sample from my yellowing notepads that I have retained over all these years:

- On Western and 109th St. Old service station. What's the gallonage? What are our plans for it?
- Check the telephones at my apartment.
- Plan my vacation. Interested in Rome. Three daughters. What's to see?
- Visit service station at Argyle and Franklin. Sign on Argyle side doesn't work.
- Write to Jon Katzenbach of McKinsey and compliment on study.
- Find out about the places to do laundry. (When he divorced and first moved into an apartment.)

How do George Getty's idiosyncrasies connect to the founding of ESPN? Amazingly well, actually. But because I frequently acted as his personal insulator to separate him from the outside world and allow him access to a certain comfort zone, I learned something about the role of relationships, both close and distant, in business communities. I often flash back to those times and think that the specific tasks I did, which sometimes struck me as ludicrous, really meant little. What really did amount to something was the opportunity for him to teach and for me to learn and follow. I learned the value of vaguely relevant detail, and that what seemed vague then might not seem so later. Such a lesson would, in retrospect, permit me to take the reins when it finally came time to spur ESPN on to glory.

Though my ego could never be classified as small, I learned under the most extreme conditions to control it and keep it to myself. I was like the faithful servant who would stand, holding a seat, until everyone had entered, and then someone else would show up. By then, the chairs were all taken, so I would stand. But the standing would often afford me a clearer view.

What seems strange to me now is that I was, all the while, tending to multimillion-dollar deals. I was a vice president of a small empire. Sometimes, given the strange requests, I'd have to remind myself of that lofty and accountable station. Several years into the successful creation of ESPN, I finally realized the significance of the lessons George Getty had given to me. I will explain later.

Getty served as a member on the board of directors of Douglas Aircraft, and he once invited me to come along to keep him company when he attended the board meetings at the Douglas headquarters in Long Beach, California. We passed a lot of the trip hashing over different aspects of the business, and he asked me for my own take on certain people and situations based on their reports. Often, I was instructed to write a letter to each of Getty Oil's division general managers requesting an update and status of their respective divisions. After they had responded, I provided Getty with a summary of five items—three sentences or fewer per item—about each of their operations. The basis for this would be couched in George's pet question: "What is cooking in each of their minds?"

With my notes, we covered a wide range of concerns as we sped down the highway in the company limousine, the windows down, the air blowing into our faces, both of us like tourists taking in the day.

In early 1967, Douglas Aircraft, builder of World War II airplanes like the B-17 Flying Fortress, and the TBD-1 Devastator, was hustling for money, and the banks were tightening credit. Things appeared gloomy, and rumors had begun to circulate about the financial condition of the corporation.

In February at the Douglas meeting, Getty was flinging out assignments to me like they were peanuts when he turned, looked at me earnestly, and said, "What do you think Mr. Getty would say if we were in the aircraft business?"

I smiled obliquely. I was not usually inclined to reserve my opinion when asked for it, but for some reason, I did so this time. I think I was shocked. My lack of response was less a matter of concern about finding myself in the middle of a father-son battle than it was a concern for being in a pragmatic business debate. I couldn't see Getty Oil Company tied up with a failing company, but what did I know? I had taken wilder flings myself and probably would continue to do so in the future.

Once we arrived at the board's meeting place at Douglas' headquarters, Getty placed a quick call to a Douglas executive and arranged for me to tour the plant while his meeting took place. As I walked into the plant, I could almost sense in my chest the powerful, resonant thrum of the giant engines: B-17s, one-thousand strong heading out over the White Cliffs of Dover. I could feel the presence of Rosie the Riveter and the others who built the planes, and of the WASP (Women's Air Service

Pilots), who ferried the planes away to locations on the way to the fronts of World War II.

After the visit to the plant, I learned that James Smith McDonnell, from McDonnell Aircraft Corporation, had tendered a purchase offer for Douglas Aircraft. The offer, apparently, was so lowball that it must have seemed more an insult than an offer, especially to a great corporation that had helped win World War II. The stunned board immediately declined. George Getty, not usually one to challenge the status quo, scrambled to his feet and asked for a vote to consider an offer from Getty Oil Company. By proposing the offer, George had placed himself—heart leading—into a dangerous conflict with his father, J. Paul Getty.

At the rest break, Donald Douglas left the room, knowing that something unusual was happening, but not confident in the direction things were taking. He spoke with James McDonnell and told him of Getty's counter offer, which must have come as a surprise. "How much is the offer?" McDonnell asked. Douglas informed him of the amount and the details. "I will beat that," McDonnell said.

The board voted in favor of the new McDonnell offer, and on April 28, 1967, the companies became the McDonnell Douglas Corporation.

We met up after the board meeting, and I could tell that George Getty was indeed proud of himself for his independent action. He'd acted *on his own*, in an unsanctioned way, forgetting his controlling father—a bold move and entirely out of character for him. After all, he had watched his brothers clash with their father over their own lives, while he had played the game responsibly, the way his father wanted, usually without moral support or the slightest encouragement. Now George, without the push and direction of his father, had done something remarkable. Although the chains connecting them had not broken, they had likely loosened, if only for an afternoon.

Unfortunately, the cold shadow of his billionaire father ultimately led Getty to seek solace in the drugs—barbiturates, amphetamines, and others—that eventually destroyed him. But on that day in 1967, Getty had made his stand in the world.

I never heard about the elder Getty's reaction to the aircraft company offer, but I often wondered what would have occurred had the younger Getty's offer been accepted. Even today, though, it strikes me, against a better part of my logical self, that the Douglas sale to Getty Oil could have happened. I don't know why I say that, except that Getty had leverage I don't think he ever used and might have felt pressed to point out in this instance. He was the only one who could run the oil company for his father. (Although ironically, some employees at the oil company who used to work for Getty had higher and more influential titles than he did at the time of his death.) Anyway, fighting in two directions to save face might have pushed him to truly confront his father—and that might have saved Getty's life.

Over the years, J. Paul Getty felt no need to be a father to his sons, and it showed in them. Paul, whose youthful letters to his dad were corrected for grammar by his father, became a heroin addict along with his wife, the beautiful Dutch actress Talitha Pol. Another brother, Gordon, had to fight his father in court over his decisions on the allocation of dividends from the Sarah Getty Trust. A classic story is told about J. Ronald who, after a time with Getty Oil, decided to embark on a career as a movie producer. This shocked his father, who inquired about Ronald's credentials for the field. Ronald postulated that the key to producing in Hollywood rested on hiring the right people, people with "know-how." J. Paul Getty said, "So you have the money and they have the 'know-how.' Well, I've no doubt they will soon have the 'know how' and the money."

Although it appeared that the patriarch's graceless, penetrating gaze would fall upon his eldest son, George, as a result of his bid for Douglas Aircraft, the wrath was shelved for later. I sometimes think of my friend, the Oklahoma football coach Bud Wilkinson, who put it so well: "The man who tries is better than the man who doesn't try at all."

George had finally tried.

CHAPTER 4

Preparation
A, B, and C

famous orator, besieged by admirers after a remarkable speech, heard a comment like this from someone in the audience: "You did a wonderful job with the speech. You must have stayed up late preparing." The orator stepped back, bright eyes blazing, and said, "I've spent my whole life preparing for that speech."

Careful listeners, especially those from the culture of American business, will stand back and scrutinize a performance. One slip and the ground becomes less firm, less accommodating. It is often a lifetime of work that enables us to accomplish great things. And sometimes one is assigned that work as a kind of test. Remember in *The Godfather* when the godfather, played by Marlon Brando, assigns his son, Michael, something to do? Through this apparently simple act, Michael gains standing—he will become the next godfather.

Preparation for playing the biggest hand of my life—the deal for ESPN—came not so much from "my whole life," which sounds a bit too grand, but from at least three major Getty projects I handled. In retrospect, I had to successfully take the long steps necessary to piece together those deals, which strengthened my position in Getty Oil. I needed all the strength I could get. I didn't want to feel as though I was buying on margin. I wanted to have control and authority.

Life is about practice—and then suddenly you're in the game.

Flashback to Acapulco, Mexico, 1939. Soon-to-be President of Mexico Miguel Aleman said to his friend J. Paul Getty, "Paul, buy property here. It will appreciate in value." At the time, the elder Getty was having an affair with actress Paulette Goddard, as well as spending time with the future president in his villa in Acapulco. Along with members of Aleman's future cabinet, J. Paul Getty purchased 250 acres of oceanfront land on Revolcadero Bay, some six miles outside the city of Acapulco. He later said that he had never seen a more beautiful stretch of beach property.

He never returned to Acapulco, but after World War II, he was encouraged to build a hotel on the site. In 1956, he had a two-story rambling hotel designed by American architects, completed, and opened for business. The manager, Charles "Buck" Rogers, was frustrated from the beginning with having to report directly to J. Paul Getty, who by then had relocated his residence to Sutton Place, a fine, old English manner house with 72 rooms situated on one thousand acres west of London. Requests from the hotel for support went unanswered, and tourism alone failed to provide the cash flow needed to keep the hotel competitive. Although Getty Oil Company owned the hotel, the hotel management reported directly to J. Paul Getty. During the midsixties, Getty informed his son, George, that because the hotel was situated closer to the company's major businesses, he was directing George to accept responsibility for the hotel and its management.

It was then that I received a major acknowledgement from George Getty. He called me to his office and, for more than an hour, gave me the history of the Hotel Pierre Marques and of contacts that Mr. Getty had made over the years in Mexico—business and personal contacts made over 30 years before. One such friend, Señora Yolanda de Castro, was the charming and well-connected widow of the former financial minister of Mexico. The elder Getty had met de Castro some years before at a social gathering, and they had remained friends throughout the years. George Getty went on to say that he had vacationed at the hotel a number of times and had spent social time with the manager, Rogers, and his wife, Dianna. He questioned their desire to manage the hotel aggressively. He then instructed me to make plans to go to Mexico. He telephoned the corporation's attorneys and requested that they meet with me upon my arrival. He had also contacted de Castro and asked if I could arrange an appointment to meet with her and discuss a matter of great importance to Mr. Getty and himself. I had never been to Mexico, and the thought of being a personal emissary of Mr. Getty's was exciting.

In Mexico City, I met with lawyers who filed the incorporation papers for the hotel. Then I traveled to Acapulco, where Getty had instructed me to act as a kind of secret witness at the hotel. Although I didn't have to don a wig and mustache to conceal my identity (no one knew who I was then anyway, really), I learned to observe and ask questions as if I didn't really care, as if nothing was riding on the answer. On the first visit, I stayed for five days, making copious notes about all aspects of the hotel's operation. I spoke with anybody I sensed might be eager to reveal some local secrets. I learned quickly that Charles "Buck" Rogers had turned the place into a private sanctuary, and when reciprocating for personal parties, the hotel became the host. As I stood looking over the place, I wondered what I could get the Gettys to do about the place. I had gone into my investigation with the knowledge that George Getty didn't really want anything to do with this romantic investment by his father—although he did like vacationing there.

"Your suspicions are correct about the hotel and management," I promptly reported back by phone to the younger Getty, unsure whether I should measure my words. He suddenly grew interested.

"I'll be down next week," he said.

"I'll go to Mexico City, and I'll find a manager," I said.

"Go ahead," Getty answered.

Two days later, I met a Swede by the name of Warren Broglie in Mexico City, who had been introduced to me by de Castro. "I have my own little hotel here," he said. I nodded. "I don't know that I need another." I hoped he felt he had overstayed his opportunities there, running his own small, but successful, hotel, and would seize the opportunity to move. He seemed amiable enough, and I could sense not only mere competence in his demeanor, but ambition. At first, he seemed reticent, as if testing the waters was his modus operandi. And so, we kept talking.

"I suppose I can bring in a resident manager here and commute."

"I'm sure that would be fine with the corporation," I said. I needed that to happen. Good people make things happen.

George Getty decided to fly into Acapulco on the 1:00 flight, and without changing his attire for the tropical climate, the two of us went directly to the manager's office. Getty reviewed the information I had gathered, added a few personal observations, and asked for, and received, Roger's resignation. The general manager acted neither surprised nor resentful.

It was obvious that Getty was feeling very good about the chain of events. Taking prompt and decisive action on something his father's negligence had allowed to drift pleased him. We decided to have dinner in downtown Acapulco. Broglie had returned to Mexico City, so I invited his newly selected resident manager, Leo Schwilling, to join us. Schwilling was a German and had experience in hotels throughout the world, most recently in Mexico City.

Following dinner, Getty suggested we go to a night club where he had been on earlier visits to Acapulco. We were all in great spirits, enjoying the many *señoritas* in attendance. Later in the evening, I noticed that Getty had been dancing and had not returned for nearly 40 minutes. Schwilling told me with a wink not to worry, as Getty apparently had run into an old friend. On future visits, I frequently suggested visits to this nightclub just in case Getty's friend was there again. Later, on a trip to Mexico City, where Getty was to meet the new president of Mexico, Diaz Ordaz, we went on to Acapulco by car, staying overnight in the posh city of Cuernavaca, where Getty met another old friend. Being the faithful companion I was, our discussions never went to those subjects. Sometime later, I learned that he had made plans to meet his friend in advance of coming to Mexico.

Shortly after Broglie took over the operation, he proved his abilities and reenergized the hotel—my discretion, then, had been affirmed. Soon the place sparkled under the blue Acapulco skies, and the maintenance department found even the least obvious problems and fixed them. I was conscious of my role there but avoided trying to interfere with Broglie, although my position with Getty as vice president of diversified services certainly gave me the authority and license to do so.

In 1966, I frequently traveled from Los Angeles to Acapulco, where I assisted in directing the renovation of the hotel. De Castro, so helpful in our search for a manager, was given the contract to redecorate and update the furnishings throughout the hotel. New lights and furniture created an ambience of relaxation. Theretofore, marketing had been guided by the concept of the "short stay." Before long, we decided to attempt to introduce the place as a resort hotel, one with all the amenities of Miami or

New Orleans and at a cheaper price. We watched as the numbers of vacationers increased, and soon the hotel became a popular destination for a large number of cognoscenti from all over North America.

An airline agreement in 1965 had opened up direct air transportation between the United States and Mexico. Previously, U.S. airlines were restricted to flying into Mexico City. From there, tourists flew to Acapulco on Mexican carriers. It was not unusual for the Mexican airlines to wait until their planes were fully occupied, thus creating great inconvenience to American visitors. I watched with barely concealed glee as Eastern Airlines began to advertise Acapulco as a top resort destination. Western Airlines began to fly to Acapulco directly from the West Coast. Clearly, the time was right for a first class hotel—and not just with spruced-up rooms, but with expanded recreational facilities and haute cuisine.

Within the Getty organization, by turning the hotel over to his son, J. Paul Getty had, once again, given his son the wrong end of an already dubious stick. To make matters worse, the old man himself, through simple neglect, had made a mess out of the hotel in Acapulco. I knew George wanted to dump the hotel. It was certainly tempting, though I wondered whether it was prudent or timely.

Then American Airlines contacted the Gettys and offered $8 million to purchase the hotel. After a round of correspondence, J. Paul Getty gave the go-ahead. We immediately arranged a meeting with the American Airlines' lawyers and executives. In most such deliberations, there is usually some room to negotiate, but this time, both parties were ready to sign the papers that had been prepared by the Mexican authorities. At the last moment, word came that Mr. Getty had reservations. He sent a telegram with the terse direction: "If they'll pay $8 million, someone else will pay more."

When the hotel was originally assigned to George Getty, it was his intention to sell it for enough to recoup the original $4 million investment.

Now, it would seem he and I stood benefit: any upcoming sale would double the original asking price. In the meantime, Getty had nearly rid himself of the burden of the hotel, but, nonetheless, would continue to have to wait. I felt a sense of discouragement because I knew what it meant to Getty to be free of it, and I also knew what it meant to have to go through the process of selling the hotel again.

On the other hand, I realized the implication of J. Paul's Getty's decision—it would, indeed, be smart to hang on to the hotel. Things were beginning to heat up in sleepy Acapulco, a destination with a metamorphosis as dramatic as a butterfly's in store. We figured that an airline might be interested in purchasing the hotel someday or, at the very least, we could enhance its desirability for a whole new generation of visitors. Before long, luxurious beds were installed in the updated, redecorated rooms. New lights created a softer, subtle enhancement, and a new paint job reaffirmed the charm of the arabesque arches.

J. Paul Getty was fond of saying that money is like manure: if you spread it around, it will make things grow. But he might have been concerned that things smelled a little too badly had he known of our plan to convince the Mexican government to grant us a permit for a new convention center and golf course. While we waited for Mexico to overcome its sluggish action on our permit, someone suggested that we could oil the creaky machinery of government by offering to pay a fee—really, a barely disguised bribe—for the permit.

But first we had to solve a problem rooted in an antiquated Mexican law, still in effect at the time. We were limited to only a 10 percent return on the total investment per year. However, if we invested more, as in our intended expansion, we could then charge more. Yet the catch remained: we still had to have that permit from the government to proceed with the expansion in the first place, and this seemed to take our efforts back to square one.

However, eventually, the offer to pay a fee worked, and we received word that we could make the capital improvements. Thus we could charge $14 more per night, a move we effected immediately. And by charging $60.00 instead of the old rate of $46.80, a fee of $50,000 would become amortized in just six months.

In business, I always looked for reasonable and fair deals for all concerned, but such deals were not so easily conducted in Mexico. We were forced to accomplish some of our projects on a tight budget and, predictably, problems reared their heads faster than irate workers could strike. People who realize they are working for one of the richest men in the world don't usually understand the concept of frugal budgets. Our workers in Acapulco figured that if someone had big money, he was required to spend it. My attempt to explain—diplomatically—that the hotel property was not necessarily a priority became challenging, to say the least. Everything was further confounded by the language barrier, and reasoned communication often seemed downright impossible.

My first assignment of any real magnitude involved building that golf course, which was to be known as the Pierre Marques Club de Golf. I knew golf only as an average player, a country club member with a handicap that perpetually hovered around 12. I had little knowledge of golf course dynamics, much less about building one. I did know that if we were to build a golf course at the Hotel Pierre Marques in Acapulco, we would need publicity and a level of attraction sufficient to lure the golfing tourist away from traditional golf resorts in Hawaii and Florida. I contacted Mark McCormick, a longtime friend of mine and the business manager for Arnold Palmer. McCormick was planning a trip to Los Angeles, and we arranged to meet at the Regent Beverly Wilshire Hotel in Beverly Hills.

McCormick, then and later, was an impressive figure. His representation of Arnold Palmer, Gary Player, and Jack Nicklaus, along with his developing company, International Management Group, was legendary in sports circles. Always focused and prepared, McCormick carried a pack of index cards and took copious notes during our conversation. I later understood why: he had phone calls and business affairs throughout the world, and his note cards were his laptop computer in those days. After reviewing our plans for a golf course in Acapulco, his interest piquéd because, at that time, Arnold Palmer had not connected himself with a golf course in Mexico. We decided that the three of us would meet at the upcoming U.S. Open at the Olympic Club in San Francisco. The plan was that we would meet Palmer for breakfast on a Saturday morning, review photos of our property and hotel, and if he was interested in designing our course, we would then all travel to Acapulco in his plane following the tournament on Sunday for an onsite inspection.

The three of us met for breakfast in the Olympic Club clubhouse. Palmer reviewed materials I had and, after further discussion, agreed to the plan of going to Acapulco following the tournament on Sunday. With that, Palmer departed for the practice range, and I looked forward to spending the weekend in the gallery watching the best professionals in the world vie for the title of U.S. Open Golf Champion. It got even better. Palmer was up by several strokes on Sunday's final day. My mind was in overdrive: I might be flying to Acapulco with the new U.S. Open champion and possibly signing him to design and build the Pierre Marques golf course.

My dream and expectations met a sobering conclusion: Billy Casper made up seven strokes on the final nine holes Sunday afternoon and was tied with Palmer at the end of the day. McCormick informed me that Palmer could not commit to the Acapulco trip because of a conflict and would have to reschedule. I later learned that, disappointed with his meltdown on Sunday, he was in no mood to do anything but return home and lick his wounds.

Percy Clifford, a Scotsman who previously had built a golf course in Mexico, the Club de Golf in Mexico City, was mentioned to me. He was described as having broad knowledge of golf course construction and was highly respected by golf enthusiasts in Mexico. He also spoke fluent Spanish. Clifford flew down from Mexico City for a meeting. He seemed to be an excellent choice for the job. We toured the site and, over lunch, discussed details of how he would proceed if he were retained. I liked what he said. Not only was he well known in Mexico, he was also a competitive golfer, having played in seniors tournaments in Mexico and the United States. We reached an agreement, Clifford moved into the hotel, and over the next couple of weeks, heavy-equipment operators began to move dirt and carve out the design of what we all agreed would be a challenging championship golf course with a magnificent view of the ocean.

Of course, troubles arose. Clifford informed me that the irrigation system for the golf course required special technical expertise. Although the fresh water aquifer was only four or five feet below the surface, it rested on a deep layer of salt water at sea level. If the salt water was breached, it would contaminate the fresh water, and the result was unthinkable: no water for irrigation, environmental chaos, and irreparable damage to the resort itself. I requested and received approval to transfer an engineer from the Getty operations. The Robert Trent Jones Company designed the irrigation system and, with man-made lakes and special pumping strategies, was able to avoid penetrating the salt-water aquifer.

Clifford hired equipment contractors whose job was to level and mold the landscape. Then, yet another stark reality: what about the grass? I felt helpless. We learned that golf course grass could not be found in Mexico that would sustain itself in the soil near the ocean in the high humidity and other adverse conditions of the ocean-side course.

Where would we find grass hardy enough? Did such grass exist? At that point, I could only imagine the worst: the "finished" golf course as the golfer's worst dream—one long 18-hole sand trap or, perhaps worse, barren fairways standing as sad and pathetic as cement sidewalks in some deserted housing subdivision. We were in our own deep bunker, trying to get out. We needed to locate a grass that would actually grow. I almost hoped the whole 80 acres of sand would up and blow away, but it, of course, did not. Not with those soft, balmy breezes that spilled off the Pacific. Were we fighting nature itself?

I could see my career with Getty taking more than an out-of-the-way turn. I imagined I might find myself relieved of my duties. I saw myself like Chuck Connors at the beginning of each episode of *Branded*, stripped of Getty insignia and turned out into the very desert I'd created. A golf course without grass? It seemed absurd, but a possibility—albeit a bumpy one. George had recently reminded me sternly of the eight-month deadline for completion of the course, and that date in October appeared like a specter with hard eyes on the horizon. And I knew that deadlines mattered a great deal in the Getty Oil corporation.

The Trent Jones people again came to our rescue. They referred us to an agronomist in Georgia, an expert in grasses and ground cover, who immediately flew to Acapulco, tested the soil and other elements, and delivered a recommendation. We should use Bermuda grass, a type of broader-leaf grass that sends out powerful rhizomes, and which, he explained, had sometimes been called upon for use in sandy areas of the South to help curb erosion. We quickly arranged to purchase enough grass to cover the course.

Two cargo planes delivered plastic sacks filled with "stolons," small sprigs of Bermuda grass. Eighty acres of sod on two C-47s seemed an unusual idea at the time, but it had to work. Nature abhors a vacuum, but she probably would despise a golf course consisting of only sand, and it certainly wouldn't attract golfers.

I felt no peace of mind as I awaited the arrival of the grass. There were no guarantees, but plenty of grass jokes. "Did you get stoned and misplace the grass?" I had nothing to do with marijuana, but it wasn't funny anyway. Finally, when I saw the large planes appear in the distance—small glints in the sunlight, winks against an unbelieving world—any confidence I had that this would work still could not bolster me. The C-47s landed eight miles away at the Acapulco International Airport, and the task of unloading began. I was anxious and wanted to roll up my sleeves and pitch in, but we had hired 80 Mexican workers—*peóns*—to unload the cargo and, to my surprise, they made quick work of it, and finished the unloading in a day. That achieved, it took about four days for the *peóns* to plug the long springs of Bermuda grass, piece by piece, into the fairways. The groundskeepers continually watered the newly planted turf, turning the earth almost into a bog until, to a delight that unfolded over a period of seven to ten days, the Bermuda grass took root and flourished. It grew like a weed—after all, that's what Bermuda grass is, a weed.

Without the cachet a name like Arnold Palmer might otherwise bring to the course, I went about searching for another celebrity, preferably a golfer, whose name might work a little magic for us in marketing and promoting the course. I had met Noni Lann, a charming lady and good friend of Roberto de Vincenzo, the distinguished golfer from Argentina. Lann told me that de Vincenzo's schedule was hectic and that taking time for a course promotion wasn't possible for him. She said, however, that she thought he would be happy to help in any other way. I inquired if we could use his picture and an endorsement in our golf brochure. After all, he was Latin: his name would surely resonate in the United States, Mexico, and throughout South America. After a short pause, she told me that he would agree to have his name associated with the golf course, but on one condition: we would have to pay him the princely, one-time fee of $50. It was a pretty good deal to be able to use the name of a man who would accumulate five PGA tour victories and more than 100 international victories during his career.

Once completed, the entire course needed professional maintenance, which in turn, required equipment as well as expertise. We purchased myriad lawn mowers, tractors, special greens mowers, and much more that was essential for the task, often at inflated prices. The Mexicans, who happened to be expert gardeners, took over from there. Soon, the entire resort location project had been completed and would stop the eyes—and sometimes the credulity—of tourists and locals alike. The golf course, really the first major seaside course in the country with 18 holes set amid small artificial lakes, would awaken the links-trotting world to our existence. Then we knew that golfers, including celebrities, would come by the hundreds to our 6,700-yard, par 72 course.

To proceed without a suitable grand opening for the monumental task as we had achieved seemed out of the question, especially in a place known for some big, wild parties. I arranged for Dennis James, the actor and television personality, to host friends from the United States and Mexico. Several weeks before the opening party, James called me with an urgent request. He was probably unaware of my continuing uneasiness about the party, a task I wanted to pull off with class, and I felt taken aback when James suggested that I hire a friend of his who was "somewhat down and out." He told me that his friend would contribute to the dinner show and then provided me with the man's phone number, so I called him.

Our conversation did not go well. In fact, I felt put off immediately, when he seemed to come at me with questions. "What kind of room will I have? Can my wife join me? Will I have a full-time driver? Will our food and drinks be complimentary?"

I could tell he'd been thinking about how well he deserved to be treated. I was left with a headache and a clear sense that the stereotype I held about celebrities—arrogant, self-serving, self-centered, self-everything—had just been reinforced. Reluctantly, probably more as a gesture of benevolence to James, I agreed that the demanding man could come and perform and enjoy the weekend.

To my tempered surprise, the dinner went wonderfully and was capped by a fine and entertaining show. I greeted James afterward, and I apologized for doubting his entertainment choice. He shook it off, and we went for martinis. I later found out that the entertainer, indeed a down-and-outer at the time, was becoming popular and soon became an up-and-comer, then a headliner. He packed audiences in at nightclubs and won over many new fans through frequent guest appearances on television with hosts like Johnny Carson. The man's name, alas, was Foster Brooks and, strangely enough, when he made it back to Acapulco, he didn't need me to give him complimentary meals anymore. Nonetheless, he chose to maintain the disheveled persona that truly had been his character when I first had met him.

Almost from that moment on, we found that the golf course changed the entire configuration of Acapulco. For Western Airlines, particularly, it opened a new horizon. Instead of making promotions for Hawaii, the airline began to usher in the era of Mexican tourism. And golf threw open whole new marketing possibilities. Clint Murchison, the Texas oil magnate, as well as hundreds of other jet-setters who could travel at will to any number of exotic, overseas locations, waxed enthusiastic about "the new Acapulco."

On the other hand, I still needed confirmation on the new golf course, so I contacted my friend, Al Mengert, a successful touring pro from my hometown, Spokane, Washington. I proposed that he come down to try out the new course, for Mengert wasn't one to mince words, and I knew he'd give it to me straight. He played the 18 holes and, at the "19ᵗʰ," told me he approved of the course. "I haven't played many courses where I had to use *every* golf club in the bag," he said of the challenge. I wanted to say—in reference to the splendid ordeal that was the making of the course—"Neither have I."

The Gettys could not toss off the fact that the golf course had attracted large numbers of tourists. In fact, the hotel sold out its rooms 100 percent of the time during the three prime tourist months each year. Expert hoteliers consider that kind of occupancy impossible to maintain, but the demand for the Hotel Pierre Marques helped us to not only cultivate a profile that fit well with the other resorts in Acapulco, but also gave us an edgy distinction. Then it became a matter of cooperating with the other hotels to arrange accommodations for the increasing flood of tourists.

As hard as I worked in Acapulco, I played equally hard. And George Getty's visits had the potential to jeopardize all I had accomplished. I needed to be on my best behavior for him, but in Acapulco, with all the lovely people flying in and out from Europe and all over the world, it wasn't easy. When Getty came down, I'd meet his late-afternoon plane and transport him to the hotel for a swim before he'd meet me for dinner. The discussions about business and fishing became the twin orders of the night. He was still relaxed in those days.

At the Pierre Marques Hotel, Getty would have a nice room—although nothing special—with a view of both the Sierra Madre Mountains and the Pacific Ocean. He would retire early, and when I was confident that he was asleep, I'd climb into the company car and head for a night out in Acapulco. In those days, social life never really got started until 11:00, so I'd pass my time until then, perhaps with a few cocktails and visiting friends. Finally, I'd head over to one of the multitude of fashionable discotheques or nightclubs. After all, in the seventies, discos were the burning rage. Light from hundreds of soccer ball–sized strobes danced with us, broke into little jewels, and scattered across the floor like stardust. Because almost all the doormen at the posh clubs knew me, I knew that if a club wasn't hopping, I could get in easily somewhere else where it was. During the years of the Acapulco project, I had made many friends and contacts, including Moe Dalitz, who, with partners, had owned the Desert Inn in Las Vegas and then the popular resort and spa, La Costa, in Carlsbad, California. Dalitz and one of his associates, Allard Roen often came to Acapulco for meetings with "friends from the Midwest and East Coast." These friends preferred to stay in separate hotels, but the Pierre Marques was always their favorite. In return for accommodating them, we enjoyed a fine relationship at La Costa.

I'd stay up until 4:00 or 5:00 in the morning and then hurry back to the hotel, where I'd sleep for two or three hours before meeting Getty for breakfast. Breakfast was always a struggle for me to appear fresh and invigorated when I met my boss. On many occasions while he was there, Getty requested that I make arrangements for him to go deep-sea fishing, with the clear expectation that I would join him. Once we had motored into the rollers of the open ocean, I would begin to feel the night before. Quite simply, I wasn't a very good sailor and, even in the best of times when I was rested and not hungover, I frequently became nauseated at sea. No sooner than when we were separating from the dock, I'd feel that old, familiar, irresistible reflex, and I'd end up bent and mulling over the sea from the side of the boat as I tried hard to hide my green face from Getty's view. I couldn't let him know that I'd been out all night. What he would have done had he found out I don't know, but I know that I lived some harrowing moments operating outside the conservative ways of Getty Oil. In many respects, I gave a premiere performance each time Getty came down to visit.

In early November, I received a letter from Getty, who was visiting his father in England. Earlier, I'd sent him a spate of photos of the hotel and golf course that I hoped he'd forward to his father. Getty explained that his father had received a goodly number of compliments "on his decision to build a golf course at the Pierre Marques in Acapulco." The letter explained that he now had "a very constructive and pleasant view." And it continued: "Since Mr. Getty nor I have ever been partial to golf courses, I think we have you to thank for encouraging us into this project."

And while coddled turtle eggs, a delicacy, and the use of marijuana were standard fare among jet-setters, I celebrated the letter with my usual drinks—three, four, five—I don't know how many. I reveled in a moment that seemed strangely akin to hitting a home run and having the team owner, who just happened to be the richest man in the world, standing at home plate with his hat in his hand. At that time, I was proud to say, "I am a functioning drinker." Five martinis? OK. For the time being, I was. I most certainly was.

Today, the Bermuda grass that I worried would not live is flourishing and has perpetuated itself with a hard-won esteem. The tough grass now provides time-honored, time-tested greens and fairways for other golf courses that have followed suit. Now Bermuda grass on any course feels like a welcoming carpet to me, woven from the stuff of my home course.

The hotel itself, the Pierre Marques, had suffered silently, without proper maintenance, for years. As a consequence, it sometimes took all the initiative and patience I had to get things fixed promptly and economically, and I felt the pressure. As wealthy clientele, having been sold on some version of Shangri-La, sweated out the night sans air conditioning in our hotel in Acapulco, they exhibited a paucity of understanding for the complexities at hand. There was no big picture. *They* were the big picture. Late at night, sometimes, I might find myself searching Acapulco for a transformer to get the lights turned on. Water was a frequent problem too.

Asking rich people to limit themselves to one shower per day because there wasn't enough water is like telling them their money isn't worth anything, or that it doesn't talk loudly enough. Ah, wherefore the power of money?

Next door sat the Acapulco Princess Hotel.

In 1968, shipping magnate Daniel Ludwig had built a 777-room hotel, which the Getty people felt good about, figuring it would spawn more business for that area of Acapulco. After all, it could only further attention to our stake in Acapulco City. Over time, the reciprocal relationship between the two hotels grew even more cooperative, a win-win arrangement based solidly on mutual respect and mutual need. Along the way, for example, we'd trade properties, so that the two hotels could have more uniform boundaries, instead of jagged edges and noncontiguous land. Over the years, we had associated in a variety of other ways. The affiliation was egalitarian and conducted as casually as one might offer an extra T-shirt to a friend at the sports club. It wasn't clear the shirt would be returned, but it didn't matter. And, of course, small favors sometimes beget large returns!

At first, the management philosophy of the Acapulco Princess was predicated on the notion that tourists came to spend time touring Acapulco, experiencing the ocean, or even learning Mexican culture. Then the Acapulco Princess built a swimming pool—a fairly good-sized one. It was clearly a draw. The Princess management soon realized that vacationers came to Acapulco to sit by the pool for most of the day, except for occasional, short ambles down to the ocean to wet some toes or for leisurely visits to a bar or restaurant to wet something else. But the lazy happiness of the pool could not and would not be forsaken, and vacationers always went back to the pool. Guests came for the blazing sun, and they intended to get it. When the Princess decision-makers realized that 777 rooms at double occupancy could really mean up to 1,554 persons, all of whom seemed compelled to migrate to the pool, they clearly had to find a place to build another pool for the next season—or suffer the loss of their customer base.

As the Getty fortune would have it—and it frequently did—the corporation owned a lovely slice of beachfront that bordered the properties of both hotels. I received an urgent call from Warren Broglie, the manager of the Gettys' hotel. He informed me that representatives of the Acapulco Princess had talked to him about the possibility of buying this particular slice of Getty property for their second pool. I asked him if he had talked to them much. He said he hadn't. He had played it cool.

"Could you set up an appointment with them?" he asked. I must say that I felt skeptical about the chances for a deal. Certainly, I sympathized about the logjam of humanity at the Princess pool, but before we had hung up, I made it clear to Broglie that, in this case, I wasn't the least bit willing to trade or sell this particular beachfront piece of property. I gave Broglie some available times and told him to confirm one of them with the Princess folks.

Then I began to conjure up strategies, and I found the conjuring invigorating. It seemed that an opportunity had arrived, albeit quickly, and that it might just be time to see how interested the Princess might be in buying the Hotel Pierre Marques.

The appeal of the Pierre Marques lay not in a unique Aztec-theme, a style that characterized the Acapulco Princess, but in the two-story hotel's homey feel. Its bungalows felt familiar to folks who regularly vacationed in the Peekskill or the Blue Ridge Mountains. Additionally, lovers inclined to the exotic who sought privacy regarded its isolation from the hubbub of the Princess an attractive feature.

I could feel my adrenaline rise as I went into high gear. I asked our architects at the firm of Langdon Wilson in Los Angeles to draw up a design for the property in question. I told them I wanted it designed around a spiral condominium and said that its 16 stories needed to hold their own against the stunningly attractive façade of the Princess. The architects' renderings were superior. The drawings would give a convincing impression that we had planned to build on the property, and their fresh lines, as blue and vital as veins, made this seem like more than a ploy.

The Princess' representatives were two lawyers. We took our places around the conference table in Getty Oil Company's offices in Los Angeles. I said, "So, you had a good discussion with Warren Broglie about the property."

"Yes, we did, and we are anxious to make another acquisition with you so that we may commence building another swimming pool as soon as possible."

"Where we would like to build the pool?" I rejoined.

"The vacant beachfront parcel between the two hotels."

"Oh, no," I responded, as I reached across the desk for the architectural design. As I opened the rendering, I said, "Mr. Getty has recently approved the construction of a condominium building on that site."

At that point, I wanted to gain complete control of the pace and momentum of the meeting. Its sudden lurch into high gear concerned me. I wanted it to slow down some. As the Princess contingent pored over the rendering like jewelers over stones, I watched their faces go blank. At that moment, I felt like a gambler staked to a fortune, and I suppose I was.

"This is really blocking our view," one said. "Is there any way we can talk you out of this?"

"No, not really," I said. "It's an interesting financial proposition to us. You know, now that Acapulco is no longer a quiet little backwater for tourism, we anticipate that these condos will be attractive and in demand." I hoped that someone would raise the ante by broaching the prospect of purchasing our hotel, but the Princess team seemed too taken aback to get beyond the apparent impasse. As the group left, I said, "I'm sorry something couldn't be worked out, and I certainly hope they are successful in identifying an alternate solution."

We now were competitors, not neighborly business associates. All that had seemed a little unreal anyway. Mom-and-pop approaches to what is really big business, while salubrious and comfortable, are rare. I began to try to think of ways I could draw them back to the table. Then I became distracted by some other business front and let it pass.

I'd come up with no idea, but I was convinced that they would, at last, conclude that they needed to buy the Pierre Marques for their own, if only to retain the integrity of the landscape and to protect their view. But the issue of the pool was still there, and, likely, its imminence had escalated. Barely three days had passed before the phone rang in my office. It was John Notter, an erudite man who held Swiss and American citizenship. He was on the board of the Princess and managed most of Mr. Ludwig's extensive holdings around the world. We agreed to meet at my office the next day.

Maybe Notter planned to offer a lot of money for the slice of condo land. I didn't know, but I had some decisions to make. I sensed, though, through his confidence, that he might have spoken with Mr. Ludwig after hearing of my meeting with his associates. Years before, Ludwig had founded National Bulk Carriers, from which he had made a fortune buying shipyards and then reconditioning tankers after World War II. People had referred to Ludwig as a hands-on manager, a person with a keen eye on the otherwise everyday and mundane aspects of his business operations, a trait that made him the exact opposite of J. Paul Getty in management style. That, in a way, endeared Ludwig to me. That we might soon see resolution pleased me. Notter and I agreed on a time to meet.

Lo and behold, when he arrived, he didn't want to spend much time on pleasantries, but came right to the point just as we sat down: "Would you be interested in selling us your hotel?"

I said, "It's always been our plan to possibly sell the hotel—it isn't really a Getty core business." John smiled and so did I. I could have feigned deafness to hear him say what he'd said just once more.

After the two parties had executed all the contracts in Mexico City, the nature of what we'd accomplished hit me: the Getty Corporation had sold the hotel for $13.5 million, or 4.5 times the maximum amount we'd once been told we could expect from the sale of the hotel and the property. Yes, we had spent some dollars in the interim, but not enough to compete with time's influence on the yield.

However, one obstacle remained before the deal could be culminated: the money had to be transferred—no small matter at that time in Mexico. I waited nervously in the bank offices for the transaction to be concluded. When the transfer cleared, I was able to relax and, following George Getty's instructions, I called J. Paul Getty.

The phone rang several times at Sutton Place before Mr. Getty's secretary answered, and I heard her say, "It's Stuart Evey, Mr. Getty."

Mr. Getty picked up the phone and said, "Yes, Mr. Evey, what is it."

"I'm reporting that we have sold the Hotel Pierre Marques, and the money is in the bank."

"Where are you?" he asked.

"I'm at the bank president's office, and everything is in good shape."

"At Banco de Mexico in Mexico City?"

"Yes," I said.

"Oh, good, that is very nice," Mr. Getty said. "That's very nice. Thank you very much. The terms pretty much what we had discussed?"

"It's $11 million in cash and $2.5 million in a one-year note."

Mr. Getty's voice suddenly transformed—probably the closest I'd come to hearing him sing. "A loan?" he queried. "Two and a half million?" Now he was not talking, he was rhapsodizing. I remember grabbing my chair.

J. Paul Getty was tickled that he had loaned money to Daniel Ludwig. This was more than a deal: it was a gift for the man with everything—a kind of rich man's dream, perhaps, to have another rich man actually indebted to him, however fleetingly. Nothing as mundane as cash, thank you very much. Credit would be more than fine. Two of the richest men in the world in an ego smash, and I had helped Mr. Getty close the whole deal—no small satisfaction to me either.

"We'll talk again," Getty said.

As I reflected on this, I knew that we'd had about every shining moment of business in one transaction. George Getty, my boss, had savored some full ego satisfaction—perhaps a better word is euphoria—not to mention a handsome and unexpected profit. My own self-esteem swung high too, and almost held me suspended there, lighter than air. For days, I celebrated and felt as though I'd never set foot on the ground again.

I realized that I had to work to stay level and grounded. I knew that my success would make it easier for me to take—and even bask in—the really big risks with Getty Oil, but I could never have anticipated that someday my $100 million checking account might be put to the test and lead me, like a celebrity-blind fan, into a deal for ESPN.

As I prepared to end my duties in Mexico, I thought of the people I met there, and I thought of the first investments coming into Acapulco from Clint Murchison of Texas, Warren Avis of the rental car empire, and many others. I thought of change, of time and of place. I had probably traveled to Mexico more than 100 times in seven years, and soon another part of the world beckoned me: Liberia.

Liberia is *B* in my ABCs of preparation. J. Paul Getty had owned a controlling interest in Skelly Oil Company, and he had a long-standing relationship with Bill Skelly, dating back to when Getty bought Spartan Aircraft Company in Tulsa, Oklahoma, during World War II, converting it from a trailer company into an air force training site. After Bill Skelly died, Getty Oil merged with Skelly. At that point, all of Skelly's nonoil operations came directly under my purview, where my colleagues and I wrestled with whether to sell the new assets or assimilate them into our portfolio. One of the assets we decided to investigate in person was located in Liberia, the West African country American freed slaves had founded in 1821. There, they set up a homeland and built it upon a bedrock of democracy. The bedrock turned out to be quicksand.

I found out that companies doing business in Liberia had better recognize the need to make some modest investment in the little nation itself. Getty's investment supported eight or ten expatriates in their attempt to build up a palm oil plantation, a financial presence that showed us as a partner. We inherited such a need from Skelly Oil, which owned a timber concession that consisted of 190,000 acres of a remarkable wood called tetra-balinium, the hardest known wood in the world. For this unique wood and its solid concept, Skelly had built a plywood plant in the town of Greenville, Liberia, to amply supply its existing company, Van Ply, with the plywood for do-it-yourself home projects, as well as for use in mobile homes. And had we known this place well enough, even with the need to register our vast fleet of oil tankers there, we might have held back. But we didn't, so despite the twin fears of sleeping sickness and river fever running through me, I traveled to Liberia with several others to make a critical evaluation for Getty Oil Company.

Each trip by a trucker to the outer limits of the concession to load a harvest of logs could take two to three weeks. Inevitably, on the trip back, the driver would manage to get lost or perhaps find places to stop and people to see. As a consequence, the plywood processing plant would just sit—a paralyzed interloper in a strange and deserted kingdom. At other times, the wood would pile up, waiting for attention.

Liberia was recognized then, as now, as one of the leading "flag of convenience" centers in the world for registering ships and, thus, avoiding taxes on foreign-source shipping income. Clearly, though, there was no parallel between registration and shipping operations in Liberia. Shipping products from the country generally worked like this: the factory would signal in advance for a ship to come and pick up a shipment—in our case, plywood. If a ship left without our order, the plywood would sit there, like just another failure, or string of failures, on the dock. Other times, the payment of big bribes required by the port manager represented the only recourse available to the manufacturer. If the plywood did get shipped to its destination in Rotterdam, Holland, the plywood market had not accepted that species of wood for plywood. Clearly, it was a situation where the problem wasn't rough edges that needed a little sanding; it was much more complicated.

After I got a good idea of how the Liberian operation had bled the company for years—and was losing about $8 million per year—I decided to recommend that the company call it quits and quickly bring this tired colossus to closure. Contacts were made to various companies thought to have an interest in assuming our position, to no avail. At a most fortuitous time, a corporate tax attorney brought to my attention the fact that foreign nonoil losses could be taken against foreign oil profits. How timely, then, that Getty Oil Company had recently participated in a major discovery in the North Sea! That was the answer: we would gift the assets of the Liberian wood subsidiary to Liberia as a gracious gesture of friendship, write off the losses against the profits flowing from the North Sea, and be done with that albatross.

Typical of so many African governments, Liberia expected its citizens to assume positions as board members in foreign corporations doing business in the country. This applied, especially, to the locals, some of whom declared themselves to be lawyers despite their complete lack of training or education in the legal field. They carried an air of authority without the substance of knowledge. The system was beyond repair: if the goal had been to confuse and to isolate, these Liberian board members accomplished it with flair. I would lie down at night in the mosquito-infested heat troubled by their presence during specific deliberations of our board and their freedom to reveal the details of these deliberations to any prospective bidder. As a consequence, I seldom felt disposed to talk openly in front of the board. But, in order to quit operations there without having our backs to the sea, we had to present our plans to the board—there was no avoiding it. After that, I would confer, in an informal way, with President William Richard Tolbert Jr. and, with the best Getty presentation skills I had, tell him in positive terms what we planned: "We've built these facilities for your country and your people, and we would now like to present the title of these assets to you."

Unfortunately, our ignorance of the wood operations, which had gotten the best of the Skelly Corporation for at least 10 years, did not extend to the president, who soon enough received word of my plan from one of our trusty local board members.

I woke to a pale, steaming, hot African morning, agitated about my decision. I had packed the night before, shortly after I learned of the oil discovery in the North Sea, which would surely captivate the oil community and drive Getty in a new direction. I thought of my plan's tax benefits if my proposition to the president were accepted. It was time to find President Tolbert.

I awaited the moment when I would meet the president and deliver my version of a gift. I was prepared to ask him about the history of his country, about its culture and contributions to the arts, but I stood outside his government office and was told simply that he was not there. "I can't get in to see the president?" I asked. "I have an appointment."

Later, the same administrative assistant returned. "He'll be right with you," he assured me.

"I just need to see him for a few moments," I said. The assistant, a man in his forties with an indecisive smile, now grinned broadly, showing a few teeth, but could not conceal his real intentions to retreat inside the building, which he did, even before I sat down.

I waited and I waited. It was now late in the afternoon of the first day. Then came the one moment I thought I had to make the deal: I would deliver a document, which President Tolbert would need to sign. I saw him appear and I moved close to him, but he jumped into the elevator and was gone. I glimpsed his car roaring, like a fallen rocket, out from the driveway ramp underneath the building.

Feeling utterly frustrated by my failure to achieve a simple goal, I collapsed into a straw chair. I intended to wait as long as it would take. I sweltered under the African sun, the heat rays dancing above the concrete. I was stuck there, in Liberia, in the deepest shade I could find, and it wasn't very deep. During the long wait—an exercise in humility or madness—I watched President Tolbert dart out one door or another, or slant down in the backseat of his car without even so much as looking, and it seemed an absurd game. People appeared suddenly and disappeared. Failure of failures, I couldn't even give away a *company*!

Who among the board members had betrayed me by communicating my plans? I did not know, but as I had been forced to wait so miserably long, I longed for a name. I wouldn't have hurt the guy; I just wanted to offer a few relevant, choice words—a satisfying vent, if you will. I waited three days before I finally decided to contact a foreign attorney, a real one, to compose the equivalent of a registered letter. The plan worked, and after President Tolbert accepted the letter, we quickly prepared to leave.

As I flew overhead, I could see the deep forests far below, and I left wondering whether it was possible—even the right thing—for anyone to carve initials into this hardest of woods and in any but the most superficial of ways.

About a month later, as I lingered at a small newsstand on Wilshire Boulevard, still cherishing the American soil on which I walked to and from my own front door, I picked up the latest *Life* magazine. I found myself instantly sobered by its cover. The photograph was a scene from the latest coup in Liberia. I felt a heavy sadness, for I realized I was looking at two members of the corporation's board of directors in Liberia. Along with President Tolbert, they had met an almost incomprehensible death, staked as they were to the ground. Though I was deeply shaken, I read the details of the coup and the story of a country being forced to make way for an animal, a military sergeant by the name of Samuel Kanyon Doe, who had overthrown the government.

By now, my path had taken me to Acapulco and to Liberia. Ultimately, it would lead me toward another major business success.

Anybody want to buy a mansion? I might just as well have hollered it out on some street corner—and been as well served. Sutton Place, the home of J. Paul Getty, chairman of Getty Oil Company, was being sold following his death in 1976. The estate was no longer required as the headquarters of Getty Oil's worldwide operations, so the decision was made to discontinue the annual expense of maintaining the property. Selling the 70-room Sutton Place mansion, or, for that matter, even couching the language for an ad, seemed foolish and daunting, maybe futile. I would recline in bed and think of how to promote its sale: "Enjoy the world beyond your wildest dreams. Relive the time of the reign of Henry the VIII in a mansion of the past." Where does one start? What do you emphasize? Let me name a few of the actual characteristics of the mansion: 56' dining room, gallery hall, 120' library, 140' gallery, minstrel's gallery. The minstrel gallery would stop me. Who knows what a minstrel's gallery is? Should I define it? Would I mention the one thousand acres of garden or not, because of the costs of upkeep? But, as they say, if you have to ask the price, you can't afford it.

An advertisement could have featured its unique Italian terracotta, not typical English stone; or the Renaissance brick with friezes, quoins, and cornices; the leaded glass; the brick gables. I could have stressed the drive to the mansion, three quarters of a mile past rhododendrons and tall trees, making for greater privacy. The 10 principal bedroom suites, indoor and outdoor swimming pools, four reception rooms, garage courtyard, 10 bathrooms, office buildings, and four separate farms. For the person who fished, it included fishing rights to River Wey. There were also 16 cottages; who had enough relatives? Who had enough lovers? I thought of J. Paul Getty, who had put up some of his lady friends, platonic or not, in some of those same cottages. It would take someone with an appetite of enormous proportions, or would it? The houses were, for the most part, separated by distance from the mansion, perfect perhaps for isolating some rock star's groupies. But, if the house didn't create enough of a reaction, the gardening surely would. The daffodil garden, the rose garden, the cherry orchard, and the well-tempered, yellow farm fields would win buyers' love and their millions.

The place was beautiful and sprawling, the structures spread out like lilies in a giant pond, following in the beauty of nature's—and man's—randomness. Who would mow the thousand acres? Flabbergasted, I realized I wasn't made for the job of selling it, but I had to facilitate it.

I decided to worry less about my sales pitch and selling points: it could damn well sell itself. The problem was how to find the right person. When we targeted our advertising to wealthy persons, thinking that the answer, it seemed like the rich jumped out of the way as quickly as if someone asked them for a loan.

Sutton Place was located in Guildford, England. The house was all-consuming, like a giant of a man with a jealous brood, for whom it was impossible to give good and full attention everywhere without enormous expense of money and time. That was precisely why it needed to be sold. The place cost Getty Oil Company $1 million per year to operate, with a skeleton staff to do the bare minimum.

And Getty Oil no longer saw any tax advantages, if they ever had realistically existed. While J. Paul Getty was still alive, he had equated his living in England to the idea of accessibility, that he could be closer to shareholders—a strange claim because shareholders lived virtually everywhere. Getty's strategy allowed Getty Oil Company to write Sutton Place into the Getty books as a business expense, which was claimed through one of their subsidiaries owned by Sutton Place Properties. To help support the claim, Mr. Getty charged visiting company executives nightly room rent, though he called for them and requested their visits. At the time, the rent ran about $50 per night, a lot of money for the time.

When Getty died in 1976, Sutton Place soon began to look like a relative come to mooch on the Diversified Operations Division portfolio list. Regretfully, I had nothing to say about the transfer and, preoccupied with other business, I let it sit there until I realized the implications. One million dollars per year to operate might not seem a lot to outsiders, but it was, and besides, we would have to sell it sooner or later. Why not sooner? I spoke with several real estate agents who handled upscale properties, and I got the impression that we should have no problems, that signed sales agreements would blow like petals across the one thousand acres of beautiful grounds. We were mistaken.

Anyone showing the place could become winded talking about all or even some of the features that made up the magnificent Sutton Place.

However, despite all that Sutton Place offered, the place had an additional drawback: the British government had designated the property as a building of architectural and historic interest. People don't summarily tear down national treasures, and it would have been illegal, not to mention immoral, anyway.

In the back of my mind, I harbored thoughts of a Saudi Sheik purchasing Sutton Place. After all, the Saudi royalty was frequently coming over to England in those days, the richest of times for them. Then I thought we could sell the estate to the C. Itoh Company, or another international company, but to no avail. It seemed that nobody wanted to assume the costs of the mansion and be out of the way from the centers of commerce. Desperate to sell the property, I agreed, with certain conditions, to sell some land on the outskirts to a developer who wanted to construct houses, a plan that was halted at the permit stage and resulted in a pesky lawsuit that I had to work my way through. We finally won.

One day, as surely as someone wandering Sutton Place might find, under his nose in the vast fields, some flower they had hunted for, I was able, through a referral from one of my partners, to locate a family in Texas that might have interest in and the wherewithal to run Sutton Place. Having recently sold their oil properties, a surplus of cash sat available. Oil money—I thought it a coincidence. The attorney had told me that a young man in the family wanted to collect art. The words, "140-foot gallery" burst faster than an expletive from me.

We negotiated through an attorney and real estate broker, then finally sold the grand place as a kind of holding facility for art. In a world where, sometimes, little attention is sometimes paid to money, I succeeded in making a deal nobody at Getty Oil Company could have quite anticipated. By now, we had reached the point at Getty where we would have been tempted to get rid of Sutton Place by any and all means possible, including giving it away—anything to remove financial burden from the books. Instead, I had been fortunate enough to engineer the sale of Sutton Place for $18 million. My personal stock was rising. Based on what was happening at ESPN, I would need it.

I might have settled back on the silver boughs and leaves of my laurels, but I was driven, and some bigger project would come. Inside, I was ready for it. I was insatiable that way. I had done preparations—A, B, and C— and I was ready for something big.

CHAPTER 5

A LOVELY BUNCH OF COCONUTS

On June 16, 1978, a warm breeze blew in mist from Pacific Ocean breakers up the black lava bluff that supported the Kona Surf Hotel on the big island of Hawaii. The patio bar was built on one of the lava formations jutting into the Pacific and had created a naturally dramatic platform on which to build the rest of the luxury hotel. A few wispy clouds flushed in the expansive blue sky above the patio, where I was enjoying a bourbon and soda, admittedly not the customary tropical concoction most visitors enjoyed sipping in this idyllic vacation setting. But this was not a vacation for either Dan Burke, my longtime friend and business associate, or myself. Burke had enjoyed previous trips to the Kona Surf when I thought we might try again to add a resort hotel to Getty's real estate portfolio. Burke was a trusted member of my team and involved in all of the Diversified Operations Division's decisions. He contributed notably over the years to the success of my division.

Had this prospective venture been located in Siberia, the deal perhaps would have involved far fewer trips. But by now we were familiar figures at the patio bar, and cocktails, both tropical and otherwise, flowed as usual in this highly charged business world we controlled. I savored the gentle evening breeze, looked out over the immense Pacific, and thought fleetingly about how I had progressed from a kid shining shoes in a rough western railroad town to the confidant of some of the wealthiest men in the world.

I ordered another bourbon. Normally, I was accustomed to wearing business suits when working in the ultraconservative environment of corporate headquarters. However, the night offered a refreshing opportunity to dress casually in light blue double-knit slacks and a short-sleeved golf shirt. But I still wore my usual boxy, gold-rimmed glasses, pinky ring, and a gold neck chain and medallion. I caught the feeling of a bon vivant as I held court for a man named J. B. Doherty.

Doherty worked for K. S. Sweet Associates, a financial investment company headquartered in King of Prussia, Pennsylvania, and he represented the owners of the Kona Surf Hotel. He knew his clients were anxious to make a deal with Getty Oil. He and I had met to continue negotiations for a possible sale. Doherty was a former marine and had that demeanor, even when outwardly businesslike and seemingly relaxed. Deal makers and banks commonly approached me with ideas and proposals, so Doherty waited for the appropriate moment and then began to explain about a man he knew, a man with a wild pitch: it involved space satellites, transponders, and an all-sports television network. By now, I thought I could anticipate just about every pitch, but this one surprised me.

As it turned out, Doherty had spent the previous several months crisscrossing the United States with Bill Rasmussen, the man with the idea. That evening I also learned that K. S. Sweet had provided the interim financing to prepare a business plan and investment prospectus to raise capital for building the actual network. I'd been a quick learner in most of my areas of responsibilities, but I realized, a bit uncomfortably, that I knew absolutely nothing about cable television, satellites, or the broadcasting industry. Fortunately, I was ready to listen to opportunities that might serve me, and the mood was certainly conducive that evening. Over time, my receptiveness and flexibility ensured that I rarely missed an opportunity, and listening bought me time to formulate responses that would put me in favorable positions.

Rasmussen had circled the country pitching his concept to no avail. He had raced to contact sports rights owners seeking commitments for programming.

When Doherty and I met that evening, the deadline for Rasmussen had come and nearly gone. The project was missing a key ingredient: a major investor who could come up with immediate cash, very big money. Doherty proposed that I meet with Rasmussen at Getty Oil headquarters as soon as possible upon my return to Los Angeles.

As the three of us sat by the deserted pool at the Kona Surf, Doherty spent about 10 minutes telling Burke and me that the satellite was the key to the entire idea and was already launched and in a stationary orbit above Colorado. Rasmussen had an option on one of the transponders, or channels, that would allow the programming to be beamed back down to Earth from a broadcast uplink anywhere in the U.S. This was exciting stuff, and I continued to listen. I sensed Doherty's genuine enthusiasm. I knew that the hotel deal was likely dead, but in light of this cutting-edge but risky new idea, buying the hotel didn't seem to matter as much as it had three hours ago. I agreed to meet with Rasmussen in Los Angeles at the Getty offices upon my return.

That evening, Burke and I sat in the large living room of our sprawling bedroom suite overlooking the dark Pacific. We shared excitement about this all-sports network idea, the futuristic talk of satellites, transponders, and sports 24/7 in the uncharted waters of that very young and vastly complicated, but irresistible world called cable television.

We spent the rest of our few days in Hawaii attending business meetings, socializing at parties in the Kona Surf's kitschy lounge, and enjoying the free golf perks typically accorded to top executives at powerful companies. During the games and meaningless parties, I kept thinking about that idea, this stranger's dream of a new, and very unusual, sports television network. Every year, I had been a season ticket holder of both the Dodgers and Los Angeles Raiders. Early on, before his passing, George Getty had introduced me to many prominent owners and coaches. In turn, through them, I had come to know many of the players. Really, I considered such contracts requisite for a meaningful corporate job, and they were certainly more pleasant than the endless compromises or dubious missions in which I regularly partook to monitor and ensure success.

On the flight back to Los Angeles from Hawaii, I looked out the window and thought about the satellite floating in the airspace above Colorado and wondered if I could see it from my first-class seat. I wasn't paying much attention to the in-flight movie, so I took out a notepad and began to make a list of people to call and from whom I might get some insight to build some working knowledge, to gain some sort of an edge for my meeting with Rasmussen.

Upon returning to Los Angeles, I immediately requested that our legal representative initiate preliminary investigations into the implications or restrictions on an oil company owning broadcasting interests. I had less than a month until the meeting with Rasmussen, and I needed a lot more information. The next task was to call RCA to confirm the Satcom 1 satellite was actually present in space, and if so, to assess its capabilities.

Al Parinello of RCA assured me that the satellite was a reality, and he even explained how it hovered in the sky over Colorado and could send signals to the entire continental United States. He told me that their research showed satellite cable television programming was the future of television. The RCA executive also confirmed that the satellite had twenty-four channels or transponders, and Rasmussen had an option, with a short window of opportunity, to access one of these transponders. I put that piece of information in the "good bargaining chip" category, now understanding that the stranger I was to meet would have an air of desperation about him, no matter how well he covered it.

On another of my highly profitable networking golf encounters, I had met Art Keylor, group vice president of the magazine division of Time Life. At the time, HBO, the cable movie channel, was a subsidiary of Time Life and had been broadcasting its movie programming from a satellite since 1975. I used my new connection with Keylor to arrange a telephone meeting with Richard Munro, the president of HBO. Admittedly, long-distance introductions are not nearly as effective as face-to-face meetings, but I was still surprised by the pessimism Munro voiced after hearing the all-sports network pitch. Munro did not think that anyone would want to watch that quantity of sports! Furthermore, because most of the initial programs would not be live broadcasts, he was even more negative about the potential for attracting an adequate audience to support such a venture.

Even with that disappointment, I was quickly gathering valuable knowledge essential for this opportunity to be secured and not left to disappear into a cloud of might-have-beens. My next call was to Ed Hookstratten, a leading entertainment and sports agent. Hookstratten represented high-profile figures like Tom Brokaw, Bryant Gumbel, Phyllis George, Dick Enberg, Vin Scully, and Al Davis, in addition to other network television executives, announcers, and sports personalities. I initially met Hookstratten through a mutual friend, Don Klosterman, former executive with the NFL's Los Angeles Rams. My purpose in calling Hookstratten early in the information-gathering process was to get his preliminary views and, most importantly, to determine how difficult and expensive it was going to be to secure executives and announcers if we were to proceed with the launch of what, at that time, was a revolutionary new concept in sports television. Hookstratten was guarded and cautious, but said if I did need him in the future, he would be available.

During the rest of the short time left until the actual meeting with Rasmussen, I carefully crafted public relations inside the corridors of Getty Oil Company because in my less-than-objective mind, the preliminary outlook for the ESPN venture was more positive than negative.

CHAPTER 6

A CRAZY IDEA

On May 30, 1978, the New England Whalers of the World
Hockey Association fired Bill Rasmussen, their communications director and radio play-by-play man. For the first time
since he was a kid, Rasmussen was out of a job and understandably
depressed. Nevertheless, the very next day, he came up with the uncom-
mon idea to broadcast University of Connecticut sports on cable satellite,
even though he knew little or nothing about the actual complex dynamics
of cable television, which was in it infancy. What Rasmussen knew a lot
about was the sports scene throughout the New England states, having
spent most of his life playing sports, selling sports, or thinking about
sports as an avid fan. His son, Scott, had inherited much of his enthusiasm, but not his fanaticism. Scott Rasmussen was the more practical of the
two men, the one who tried to bring a sense of realism into their conversations, and the one who attempted to make financial sense of the elder's
schemes despite all of his father's efforts to persist no matter what the cost
or toil on human stamina. Bill Rasmussen's vision of having Connecticut
sports on cable actually materialized, but it was only part of his dream.

After the initial run, a group of local cable broadcasters was assembled,
but that meeting was less than successful. Not one of the professionals

believed the concept amounted to much. Scott Rasmussen is reported to have said with some chagrin, "At first, we thought people would try to steal the idea . . . then instead of stealing it, they laughed at us."

The grand idea still had no name. Bill Rasmussen wanted something that said *both* sports and entertainment, though at present the team had neither on board. The brainstorming session continued until he came up with "Entertainment and Sports Programming Network"—ESP for short. By the end of that evening, the father and son had devised an entity called ESP-TV.

After mostly fruitless meetings with local cable operators, Bill Rasmussen called RCA about satellite costs and the sticker shock set in. In their $100-per-month office rented to them by United Cable, Rasmussen and company attempted to build a network out of thin air. At their first press conference, only four reporters showed up, and most of them made negative remarks about what they heard, claiming it wouldn't work, was an ill-advised idea, and most importantly, that no one would watch sports on cable.

Undeterred, Bill moved to incorporate ESP-TV with a pro bono lawyer and a $91 filing fee, from the group that was flat broke. The friend who got the attorney was made president, while the Rasmussens were both essentially relegated to vice president positions. Bill Rasmussen maxed out his credit cards and borrowed from family friends to keep the new company afloat. The relationships, connections, and chemistry began to have positive influences on the turn of events when the entrepreneurs met up with RCA satellite salesman, Al Parinello.

The Rasmussens met Parinello in United Cable's spacious conference room, dressed in their finest business attire. Perhaps because of the upbeat atmosphere, the father and son didn't realize that Parinello was a desperate man too, having gone months without successfully enticing new clients to buy time on the satellite. His bosses at RCA were beginning to wonder about their own investments in this future technology and continued to put pressure on their best salesman to come up with better results in a reluctant market. In the big room sat three desperados, each playing his best hand of poker, trying to bluff the other into a deal with time on their own side. The Rasmussens gave their pitch on the ESP-TV concept, after which Parinello detailed first the capabilities of the satellite and then the cost of buying time on it. A moderate buy would cost $1,250 per night for five hours, seven days a week. The father and son did not have the cost of one night, never mind a week or month. Bill Rasmussen saw his dreams flying out the window and all hope with them. He remained calm, cordial, and even friendly as the meeting ended. Almost out the door, Al Parinello revealed another option: RCA actually had a second transponder, which had 24-hour signal capability on a year-round basis. It cost just $35,000 per month with a five-year lease.

The next day, Bill Rasmussen called Parinello in New York and told him they had a deal. The men were ecstatic. The application was immediate, and the first payment was not due until 90 days after the contract was signed.

Timing was indeed everything: shortly, *The Wall Street Journal* ran a story predicting the rosy future of cable due largely to the satellite links such as Satcom 1 at RCA. Al Parinello was now the most sought-after salesman in the business, with companies such as Time, Disney, Warner Brothers, and 20th Century Fox hounding him for space. Everything was allocated on a first-come, first-served basis, and because ESP-TV had already done the paperwork and placed an order, its interests were assured a transponder. When the "winners" were announced, media executives in Los Angeles found themselves asking, "Why didn't we apply earlier and get there first?"

"OK, now what?" was the question Bill Rasmussen asked himself. Where was all this money going to come from? Neither he nor anyone of his acquaintances had access to that kind of cash. Now that they had the satellite time in place, they needed contracts with sports teams to broadcast their games. They needed a television studio and announcer talent. They were looking at millions in start-up dollars.

While Bill Rasmussen tried valiantly to meet with NCAA officials and others, he and Scott convinced their friends at United Cable to help them find cheap space for a studio in the area surrounding Bristol, Connecticut. At about the same time, the two met with J. B. Doherty of K. S. Sweet. Doherty convinced his company to ante-up $75,000 for ESP-TV and to mastermind the prospectus to attract other investors.

The money to begin the enterprise was estimated at $10 million. And while it was up to Doherty to find such funding, the senior Rasmussen worked on his idea for the unifying theme of the sports broadcasting entity—a television sports headquarters with live announcers competing with network news—which he called simply "Sports Central."

On November 17, 1978, ESP-TV aired its experimental telecast for the first time, broadcasting a University of Connecticut basketball game and a soccer event. Across the bottom of the screen was a banner asking viewers to call in and let the network know their location. All in all, 850 households watched from 26 different states, proving that the satellite system was working perfectly.

Bill Rasmussen was convinced that people would watch sports on cable, would respond to multiple hours of sports broadcasting, and, above all, that his idea of all sports all the time was viable.

CHAPTER 7

TIMING IS EVERYTHING

Situated at the corner of Wilshire Boulevard and Western, the Getty building stood like a reminder of tasteful modesty—or perhaps it was frugality—that comes sometimes with old wealth. Just up the street was the Ambassador Hotel, where Robert F. Kennedy was shot and killed. I would walk past and think of the tragedy that ruined a nation's optimism. I had been part of that optimism. About that time, I was busily negotiating the purchase of four nearby houses for Getty. The enclave, we hoped, might help insulate us from the restless, dangerous world out there, or at least throw up a wall or a moat.

I had tried to pay attention to countless ideas in my role as head of Diversified Operations at Getty Oil, and I was rather expecting another so-so presentation when I met with Bill Rasmussen. After all, I had seen some major promoters—and promotions. In fact, I had just completed a year and a half on a project with golfer Jack Nicklaus. Getty had what was called an "agreement to agree" with Nicklaus, whereby we could have the right of first refusal in the building of housing associated with Nicklaus-designed golf courses. Though we worked well together, we never said yes, due mainly to the high interest rates, 16 to 17 percent at the time, which made the sale of housing relatively unprofitable.

I knew in advance that Rasmussen was interested in developing a television cable network. J. B. Doherty of the investment firm K. S. Sweet had told me about it during our meeting in Hawaii. I began to consider who could sit in and evaluate the proposal, ideally someone with a good knowledge of television. I immediately thought of Wendell Niles. Niles' children were in school with my daughters, and he had been a place-kicker at the University of Washington during the Hugh McElhenny and Don Heinrich record-setting days. With the number of touchdowns they made, Niles was a very busy kicker. He was also associated with NBC as a producer and later formed his own production company in California. When I called him, he graciously agreed to sit in on the meeting. He came to my office early, and I was pleased to learn that he had some knowledge of this new media, but like me, this would be his first exposure to someone who had more than a passing knowledge of it.

I also knew that Rasmussen had already made his proposal to more than a handful of telecommunications and media corporations. No one had bitten yet, apparently because no one had any interest. With that fresh in his mind, he couldn't be too optimistic, given the last stop on his fundraising mission was a major oil company that had agreed to listen to his pitch. On December 11, 1978, I got to my office before 8:00 and thought through some potential areas of discussion. Wendell Niles joined me and we chatted for several minutes. My secretary then escorted Bill Rasmussen into my office. He appeared comfortable and confident as he accepted an invitation for coffee, and I introduced Niles. We had a brief exchange about J. B. Doherty and his request that we meet, and Rasmussen expressed his appreciation for the opportunity. He then began his presentation of the basic concept of a satellite cable sports channel.

"What will it cost to launch your idea?" I asked.

"I am seeking $10 million," Rasmussen said.

"What would that include?" I asked.

"That would include trucks, hiring management and employees, starting a broadcast center, and leasing a satellite," he said. I noticed that he had a pad of paper and was doodling a crude illustration of how the satellite and broadcast signal would work. He drew a satellite Earth-station dish on a truck or broadcast center uplinking the broadcast signal to the RCA Satcom I satellite, which then transmitted the signal back to an Earth receiving dish at a cable operators' location, which, in turn, transmitted to cable subscribers via cable or microwave..

"When do you need the money?" I asked.

He paused for a moment and then gave me a date approximately one month away. "Unfortunately, too soon. I need a commitment within three weeks."

"That's kind of a short stroke. I don't think that's possible," I said, a little bit suspect of propositions that might tend to push one into something too soon. "You know how corporations move," I tossed off, possibly to soften the blow.

"My option on the transponder will expire on that date, and without the transponder, there is no network."

"Transponder?" I said.

"Yes, a transponder on Satcom 1."

"That's RCA, isn't it?" I said, trying to sound half intelligent about a subject that I knew little or nothing about. But I could tell that Niles was there learning along with me. He gave himself away with moments of cautious reaction. I kept anticipating and hoping that he would notice some discrepancies or help focus the questioning. I sometimes invited guests into important meetings to hear what I was hearing. In this case, we may have been hearing the same thing, but that didn't mean much because I was clueless.

Nevertheless, I was impressed with Rasmussen, a very good pitchman. He did the concept proud. And there was a superficial clarity that had come from his having made the pitch before, but why should I hold that against him? He seemed thorough and anxious to answer any and all questions. I admired his candor, and his reasoning seemed solid, as far as it went. He said he had spoken to the NCAA, which seemed a good first step toward having sufficient programming. That he didn't seem inclined to pull punches was another plus. He detailed his failures, including the proposed deal for the package of University of Connecticut sporting events, and that indicated something about his personality to me.

"Where's this going to be seen?" I asked.

He may have changed direction here, zigzagged even, though I don't recall for certain, but he didn't get into the attendant realities of this new business—namely that very few cable operators were equipped to receive the new satellite-delivered programming he proposed.

In retrospect—and hindsight is 20–20—I believe that if my home had had cable at the time I would have known more about it and thus felt more comfortable during the deliberations. In actual fact, and I didn't know this at the time, cable television did not exist in Los Angeles until sometime later, after the launch of Satcom 1. During that period in the late seventies, cable only served those areas across the country that couldn't receive over-the-air television, and even then, the system had limited capacity. But as Rasmussen talked, I figured satellite could reach every home in the country. I also didn't know we would later find reluctance among cable operators to spend money on the latest systems that would have greater channel capacity. Neither did I know that the cable operator needed to download the signal at an Earth station and then transmit it to subscribers who were connected to the cable operator's system by either cable or microwave.

Looking back, I feel almost certain that I might have whisked Rasmussen out of the office—or not even invited him in—if I'd known *anything* about cable. Anything.

Truly, ignorance is sometimes bliss.

But Rasmussen was invited, and I was intrigued with what he was saying. Traditionally, sports rang a bell in the minds of a good percentage of men (and today, happily, with women too), and I was always into sports. The first president of ESPN, Chet Simmons, later called me a "jock sniffer," which was a bit of an exaggeration of my love of sports and the fact that I had forged many relationships in sports long before I first met him. ESPN would not have been born, at least not with Getty as midwife, without my strong interest in athletes or the sports they played. To me, sport is a dimension of many things. It's what writer George Garrett, a boxer in his younger days, learned in the ring: "how to relax in action." Garrett captured the essence of sports in his description of one boxer's fighting as the "immemorial stalking dance." Every sport has its own dance.

I always looked for real competition in business, and nowhere could the essence of competition be more concentrated than in sports. What Rasmussen was proposing reminded me of gamesmanship, but hopefully not of the frustrating variety that comes along once in a while in a poorly executed game where *nobody* deserves to win.

Rasmussen was a good speaker, fluid with ideas, glib, and well dressed—and I found myself seduced and drawn to the concept. I appreciated his interest in providing me with tangible materials and sensible information. I sensed an occasional edginess about him, behavior one might otherwise explain away as nervousness, that I later recognized as bordering on desperation. I learned later that Rasmussen had hit the maximum on his credit card limit. If I didn't go for his proposition, he probably had no other place to go that had any real backing power, and as a result, the plans for a sports network were likely dead.

I believed in sports: did I believe in cable television? I couldn't commit to his proposal yet. I always liked to be in charge, and I wondered if it was wise for me to act when I knew little or nothing.

Rasmussen had the voice of a born entrepreneur—good, bad, or indifferent. And that was a language I understood. He had ultimately postured his presentation as if to say, "We'll build it and they'll come"—with apologies, of course, to *Field of Dreams*. But he needed the money, and I liked the financing method he outlined. He explained to us that the sports network would be supported by advertising, and because I had participated in decisions on many agency presentations, I comfortably understood the vital role of advertising.

We ended the meeting, and Niles and I rehashed some of the points for a few moments. Then he left. (Wendell Niles later got involved in celebrity tennis and produced many successful celebrity tournaments around the world, including an annual tournament in Monaco, sponsored by Prince Rainier and Princess Grace.)

Lurking in me was a passionate need to pursue this idea. I didn't know where it would lead, but I immediately called George Connor, manager of finance in my division. "George, I've got something . . ." We openly discussed the merits of the project, and I found his comments encouraging.

In the days after that meeting, I sometimes left work and headed down to the Wilshire Country Club in the posh Wilshire District. There, I would have the usual number of drinks—two or three or four—and could bounce the idea of ESP-TV off friends or acquaintances: a lawyer, doctor, businessman, or even a Hollywood mogul. They each offered an opinion. And they knew with a Getty man they didn't have to be protective of their wallets. I liked the exchanges for more than the advice I'd receive. It's difficult to explain, but I wanted to keep as many people informed as possible so I could feel like I was in the game. I needed to keep my energy up and stay positive about the ESP-TV proposal. Even if the reviews came out negative, I would not be swept away with criticism, for I knew I could rationalize—at least at first—this flirtation with the concept of an all-sports network. After all, practically everyone in my circles turned out to know little or nothing about satellite cable. How could anyone consider me ignorant for taking a leap of faith, a blind one at that, if he or she knew as little as I did?

Glenn Davis became a third ear for me. Frequently, I'd run into him at the country club, and he would sit as if he could see my ideas take shape. Davis was a sports legend, a longtime friend, and a golfing partner. In 1946, he had won the coveted Heisman Trophy during his playing days at Army. "Mr. Outside" was the nickname for this once-speedy running back, a man who had the knack of running outside for touchdowns. Along with Felix "Doc" Blanchard, "Mr. Inside," they formed a formidable duo. In a sense, he and Blanchard represented dual metaphors. In other words, I could run inside or outside in my approach to the Getty board. For the moment, I was thinking inside. I would confront the board directly with what I was becoming more and more confident I would be doing. All the while, I think Davis never showed annoyance, only a kind of inward sympathy. He seemed to know I was fighting an uphill battle on this one, but he always served as a good and patient listener.

One day, Davis leaned over to me in the lounge and said, "You're going to work yourself out of a job if you keep doing this ESP-TV thing." I think I neglected to think much about that comment at the time, but I certainly did think about it later.

Some days passed. From my office on the 18th floor of the building, the world was open before me. I had anything but a stiff-necked view of the world or its possibilities. Seated there, in my leather, high-back chair, I felt myself drawn more powerfully to the idea. I don't know if there was a triggering moment, but I would stare out at the skyline and fret about the status of ESP-TV and the endless amount of due diligence that needed to be accomplished if we would proceed. Sometimes I would scarcely notice the metropolitan skyscrapers of Los Angeles, including the Arco Towers, the Bank of America, and the Chandler Pavilion, where the Academy Awards were held; nor would I take in, to the south, the place where building growth suddenly stopped and the deceptive blankness of the ocean began, some 20 miles away. Anyway, the thick smog would have precluded such a vista. But on a good day—and there were those where I felt especially optimistic about the ESPN future, unfettered by the negative—I could peer toward the San Gabriel Mountains to the east, in Pasadena.

Timing was everything. I half rejoiced in Getty's recently expressed interest in alternative investments, which included—albeit down on the list—a mention of television. Television ranked lower than such things as insurance and reinsurance, which soon became reality.

Soon, Getty Oil would exercise the option, and the idea would come into even sharper focus. During the months since I had first heard of the venture, ESPN had me on the edge of my seat like an impatient fan. Now, I was a player. I purchased a satellite dish and had some technicians anchor it to the roof of the Getty Building. This enabled me to invite in the wacky world of early ESPN programming. I could never really imagine what would show up next, and it usually wasn't commercials. Frequently, I looked beyond the odd programming—curling, caber tossing, field hockey, sumo wrestling—for new sponsors who could mark any positive trend toward future revenues. What I saw or didn't see was the stuff of despair, sitting there like a kind of melancholy, true believer running on the fumes of faith.

Years later, I recall someone asking if we had heavy-lady wrestling on ESPN in those earliest days, to which I replied, "I don't believe we had programming that good, to tell you the truth." At some point, the programming had evolved to where one just *had to love sports*! Luckily, I did, but ESPN's coverage tested even me. Then, too, I needed to talk to Bill Rasmussen soon about something important.

CHAPTER 8

REASONS FOR NO-ING

Most people can find more reasons to say no to something than to say yes. But the naysayers, the entirely rational (if that type of person really exists), don't always have the final word. Don't get me wrong. I believe in research. When the concept of due diligence is applied, one can make informed decisions. Still, plenty of reasons to decline buzz around in the head like bees threatening to sting your brain if you don't say no.

The book *Negaholics: How to Recover from Your Addiction to Negativity and Turn Your Life Around* discusses what to do when negativity arises within oneself. Its author, Cherie Carter-Scott, talks about how "voices" in one's head speak in disparaging ways that can stop one cold. She suggests identifying these negative voices in order to "manage them." I might have found her book handy when I attempted to put together the ESPN deal and monitor its operations.

In the case of ESPN, I was privy to numerous rationales, excuses, and what passed for reasons from the people around or from my own always-swarming inner "bees." Get it straight: ESPN had no precedent. Even more compelling, paid sports on television, in their various forms, had always faced strong skepticism among the potential sources of programming—the colleges and the professional sports organizations. That conventional attitude was, by no means, new. Ray Gross wrote in the fifties, "As to that . . . great drawer of paying audiences—sports—heated arguments are still raging about TV whether it is an ally or an enemy."

Gross goes on to point out that early efforts at telecasting college basketball and football, a few select prize fights, and minor league baseball, affected the gate receipts of various events. But while the leaders in sports promotion hid within their organizations and did nothing, an "experiment," if you will, allowed one college football game per Saturday. Nonetheless, the NCAA barred carrying the game in any close proximity to the contest's venue. In other words, if a fan could travel there, the broadcasts constituted a threat. The big pie, as conventional wisdom envisioned, was only so big. There wasn't enough to go around. Branch Rickey, who made penury a kind of art form, said, "In 10 years' time, or sooner, there will be no minors [minor leagues] unless we solve the television problem."

Though involved parties, including Getty Oil, agreed to provide ESPN service free to cable operators in the beginning, the issue of whether sports should be broadcast on television seemed to go beyond the nature of the purchase agreement, and to question whether sport itself could weather any lost attendance. The statistics from the research toward resolving such matters were, at first, less than thorough and, hence, less than definitive.

One year, the NCAA issued a report about collegiate sports attendance. The report quoted attendance revenues at collegiate football games at around $106 million in 1949; $103 million in 1950; and $98 million in 1951. Though the NCAA regarded television as a serious competitor and had made efforts to control it, gate receipts were nonetheless down some $5 million, a significant piece of that shrinking pie.

The results occasionally indicated, rather optimistically for ESPN, that confining game exposure to attending spectators and sportswriters might not be so productive. In an early experiment from 1954, Community Television Systems, which had connected 614 television sets, managed to subscribe 148 of them to Paramount's International Telemeter Company for a big sporting event. Ninety-seven percent of their viewers opted to pay for the television viewing of the USC–Notre Dame football game that year in which Notre Dame won 27–13. The Telemeter gamble, though it operated differently, was a lot like the cable model that later evolved and threw first-run films into a growing mix of programming.

From my lofty view at Getty, some of the information that I personally gleaned seemed like old history, but considering the dearth of scientific data compiled and interpreted, exploring just about anything seemed relevant. After all, we had so little history for what we were undertaking, I'd take anything I could get. How does one learn from the past when there is no past to speak of? And how does even amorphous potential take shape out of pessimism? Indeed, I was feeling pessimistic as I awaited the McKinsey Report, an analysis of the viability of a satellite sports cable network by McKinsey and Company, where people taught to assess these things would present their recommendations about the possibilities for ESPN. I anticipated that their approach would be practical, not burdened by a natural inclination to say no.

In later years, pay television had notable successes, primarily for major heavyweight boxing events. No question, people liked sports. (At times, I was beginning to wish I didn't, as I paced my office anxiously.) And though Bill Rasmussen had the instincts to pursue the NCAA, we needed a higher echelon of quality sports programming—well beyond Connecticut. Other venues and organizations—some professional—would need to be explored, including the National Football League and the National Hockey League. And if they all could be encompassed within a 19-inch set, we would have a new world before us.

But the old perceptions about television and sports were entrenched and seemed to be the hardest things for me to overcome. Certainly, too, the fact that Richard Munro, the president of HBO, and other industry leaders—experts in a new field—were unenthusiastic (or perhaps had a built-in bias) seemed to substantiate some of the prejudices weighing down on me. Or perhaps it was simply their bias about sports in general. No one can know. That old, conservative idea that someone in business should stick to what he or she knows had stirred up those bees in my head. Despite their angry thrum, another inner voice was saying that in a world where nobody seems to really know anything, a man with a dream and a bit of rational argument might still be king.

Then, of course, the exigent limits of current technology forged an argument that offered me a good way to settle down comfortably on a no-decision: the technology didn't work well enough yet. What did we really know about satellite-transmitted television? What if the satellite crashed? Being a somewhat new innovation, there was a fear that these large Earth stations sending signals to satellites would be a source of radiation. Because Bristol, Connecticut, was a small, rural community, this concern was raised with the installation of these giant Earth stations on the ESPN broadcast center site. This led management to hire Jim Black, a top engineer from Scientific Atlanta, the manufacturer, who testified that radiation from the Earth stations associated with the satellites was not the risk local authorities had envisioned. The sky wasn't falling. Bristol would be safe. Still, not much was known about the effects of radiation. I worried about rampant litigation if a worst-case scenario regarding the effects of radiation ever came to pass. Legal issues are all part of the game and—though I've been involved in my share of legal disputes—I didn't want to bring Getty Oil Company into a mess that might make some of today's landfill disputes look small. Witness today what irrational fears and unjustified timidity have done to nuclear energy in this country and you get the idea.

I heard repeatedly that I'd lose my job at Getty if I said yes to the proposal for ESPN. Some of my friends believed that ESPN's foreseeable liabilities would reach a point where I would have to go. Others didn't give me that long with Getty. My inner voice told me that certain things come along only so often, and that there's risk associated with even the seemingly mundane profit-making ventures.

Among other reasons to say no were the networks. I was reminded repeatedly that the networks held too much power and that they wouldn't permit an exercise like this to threaten their dominance. I kept thinking these sleeping giants would awaken with the thunder of a raised fist to smash and scatter the whole ESPN vision. My inner voice answered that one by saying—repeatedly as if it were a vain effort to convince me—that ESPN would not be competing head-to-head with the big networks. Rather, satellite cable sports would forge its own audiences, entirely new ones, maybe workers with different schedules who worked night shifts, or couch potatoes and Monday-morning quarterbacks who couldn't get enough. Athletes, trainers, and coaches who clamored for something more than last week's game film or newspaper statistics might be core viewers. It was all so speculative and, as I think about it now, so intangibly hypothetical. Much of what we thought was foolish. Who knew better?

I was told a few times I was whimsical to even entertain such a notion. And whimsy in business is to be avoided at all costs. But I didn't feel whimsical. I tried to exercise caution, to learn all I could. Yet I was sweating bullets, and I would continue to sweat bullets from the time Rasmussen brought the elementary concept to me in 1979, through ESPN's ongoing operations, until I left in 1983. I wouldn't really call that whimsy. Still, some people looked down at me with the kind of condescension reserved for those especially enamored of the ladies and, thus, their attached lack of reasoned discernment. I was in love with sports (as well as with the ladies), but I didn't think of anything I was doing in those days as whimsy. I was tough-minded and often demanding, even overweeningly so. Maybe some people out there even wished that I was less demanding and more whimsical.

The concern that we could not attract professional staffing or top-flight, bona fide talent also weighed heavily on my mind. We had to entice them to come to Bristol, Connecticut, yet the money was pathetically short and the locale—well, let's just say it wasn't Las Vegas. We were a speculative venture. How would they know we'd be there next week? Why would they risk it?

Maybe the world stays balanced because of the bounteous reasons to just say no. But I was going to go forth. I think I knew that inside me. Call it a man thing. Men are often accused of racing on ahead, like we do when we want to go someplace and refuse to stop and look at the map. Men are risk-takers, and that's a fact. I do believe that we sometimes have to pursue business opportunities with an unyielding, unstoppable resolve. We may fail, and we may be stupid about it, but we are going to give it the hearty college try, hopefully our best and truest shot. We'll put ourselves in a position, after a time-out for thinking, to set the court, to station our players with a strategy to win. ESPN, I realize now, may have been like that with me.

I knew that I didn't study nearly hard enough in college, but with ESPN, I would get another chance. I studied hard, preparing for a test of sorts. I labored hard. Only I was at the Library of Commerce, and I needed to get all of the information in my head. Finally, though, after I had studied and studied well, I went forth to the test. That was where I was. Because ESPN had involved studying, lots and lots of studying and rumination and reflection and waking dreams—not all good.

Ultimately, the plan might go on, blithely some might construe, or at least without regard to the rules and conventions of American business. If it did, I would risk forever being the Bill Buckner of cable, watching the ball scoot in slow motion between my legs, the ball that I had failed to corral in my glove, an error for the world to see. Or ESPN would be something special, something glorious, and I'd tap the bag with my left foot and jump into the air off my right.

CHAPTER 9

RASMUSSEN MEETS THE GETTY BRASS

hat are you feeling about introducing Rasmussen to the big guys?" someone asked me in the hallway at the Getty Oil Company.

"I don't have a problem with that," I said. What little I knew about Bill Rasmussen tabbed him as well-spoken and knowledgeable. He had a winning smile and an interesting idea. That should carry the day, I thought to myself.

But in an executive council meeting the week before, where I had summarized the investment opportunity to senior Getty management, the members suggested that Rasmussen meet and spend some time with our chairman, Harold Berg. I had to make the meeting happen. Swept up in the deadline over the satellite, I pondered how I would manage to get Rasmussen together with Berg. I had faith that if I could get them together before the satellite option expired, it would seal the deal between Getty and Rasmussen for ESP-TV, which would later be called ESPN.

I also knew that Berg, a sports enthusiast and former college athlete, would offer a sympathetic ear as quickly as he might have given a shoulder to a limping athlete during his college days. The only thing that portended easier discussion than generic talk of the weather was that of sports—unless it was the weather the day of the big game. Sports was a language we used in the corporation; it brought out a rich understanding of our own losses and, by enabling us to count our own victories, gave us that adrenaline we needed for the long march toward another major project.

Though meeting Rasmussen and subsequently approving the ESPN proposal was within Berg's authority, I knew that his comfort zone, as well as mine, would be enhanced if we could expose this high-risk investment to as many of our executives as possible. Berg respected the board of directors, and any opportunity to make them aware that we were considering this far-out investment would be to his advantage. There was a certain pattern of civility or collegiality to his decision-making, and while he did not fear making decisions, Berg liked to bring others into the circle.

I knew that we had to arrange a meeting somehow. I hoped for a small crack in Berg's schedule, but he was a busy man, and few times remained open for the kind of give and take I thought might be required. I queried him several times about his availability or any change in schedule. It didn't look good. I knew that Getty revenues had started on a downward slide and, while the corporation was clearly not in trouble, warning signs like that have a way of drawing key management away from other, sometimes newer, aspects toward the what-are-we-doing-wrong scenarios.

One day, Harold Berg stopped me in the hallway and said, "Maybe I could meet this Rasmussen guy in connection with the visit to the Oil Museum." Berg was to attend a dinner at the East Texas Oil Museum. I was surprised and delighted that my pestering had worked.

"You're going down there?" I asked, shuffling to a stop, delighted by his interest.

"Yes, we're dedicating an exhibit," he said.

"Are you going alone?" I asked.

Former chairman of ESPN Stuart W. Evey.

Here I am as a young man, age 22, receiving a certificate of achievement for outstanding advancement during training. It was after my years in the service that I went to college and then began a career in the oil business.

J. Paul Getty and me in England in 1972, not long before his son's tragic death.

The Getty Building and Universal Studios in 1984.

Meeting with the president of Mexico, Gustavo Diaz Ordaz (second from right), in 1972. George Getty is third from the left, and I'm on the far left.

Horse racing was one of George Getty's real passions in life. He owned many horses, and I would often report back to him when one of them came home a winner. Here I'm at Santa Anita, pictured with (lower right, from left) Bill Petersen, Robert Strub, and world-class jockey Willie Shoemaker.

A portrait of George Getty taken in 1956. Photo courtesy of Bettman/Corbis.

Signing a contract with Jack Nicklaus in 1977.

Signing a contract in the Getty/MCA Building in 1981. From the left, that's Sidney Petersen, myself, Sid Sheinberg, and Lew Wasserman.

Chet Simmons and I pose for a picture outside of the Bristol headquarters in 1981.

From left, that's Fred Pierce (president of ABC-TV), me, Elton Rule (president of ABC), Chet Simmons, Mike Milardi, and Scotty Connal.

My wife, Mary, and myself seated at the command post prior to an NFL Primetime *airing.*

ESPN's headquarters in Bristol, as it looks today in its 25th year. Photo courtesy of AP/Wide World Photos.

"No, John McCabe and our wives, and we plan to pick up Harold Stuart in Phoenix on the way to Midland-Odessa. Look at our itinerary and contact Rasmussen to see if he can meet us at our plane at the Van Nuys Airport.

"I'll call Stuart and give him a heads up that we are looking at an investment opportunity in television, and the principal will be on the plane with us," he said, before making his way down the hall, intently shuffling through a ream of papers.

What a break, Berg and Stuart with Rasmussen in the confines of our corporate plane. Stuart, a lawyer by trade, was a member of Getty's board. He had married a daughter of Bill Skelly, founder of Skelly Oil, now a subsidiary of Getty Oil, and was more than the sum of himself and his heiress wife. He was a distinguished and bright man on his own, a person involved in his community, and active in organizations like Ducks Unlimited. I reasoned to myself that an interest in ducks implied he had some interest in sports—in this case, hunting. A former undersecretary of the air force, he had played a role in the decision to locate the Air Force Academy in Colorado Springs, Colorado. Finally, he was our resident telecommunications expert on the board, having had some involvement with some sort of small media operation—possibly cable—in Tulsa, Oklahoma.

Harold Stuart was a close, longtime friend of Harold Berg, and if there was anyone he would use as a sounding board on this or another project, it was "Oklahoma" Harold. A smile and nod from Stuart would ice the deal. On the other hand, I wondered if his experience in the media had soured him on the emergence of satellite cable in telecommunications. At that moment, I couldn't help but think of Wendell Niles, the young resident expert from my earlier presentation meeting with Bill Rasmussen.

Berg called me that afternoon to tell me he had arranged to pick up Stuart, and that they both looked forward to meeting Rasmussen. I phoned

George Connor, my due-diligence guru, who immediately called Rasmussen. Conner reached Rasmussen at the NCAA offices in Kansas, and Rasmussen quickly agreed to catch a flight and join us in Van Nuys for the flight to Midland-Odessa and a limousine ride into town. "It's the best shot we have," I told Connor to tell Rasmussen.

Then it hit me: Getty, the little engine that could do anything, just might not.

Piling onto the lap of luxury in the Getty Oil Company jet, I joined Harold Berg and his wife; John McCabe, Getty vice president of exploration, and his wife; and Bill Rasmussen—along with an empty seat for Harold Stuart. Occasionally, I'd glimpse at the empty seat, which waited like an oversized whoopee cushion, with the same potential to sound off or embarrass.

During the flight to Phoenix from Los Angeles, which lasted approximately an hour, Harold Berg and Bill Rasmussen talked about the project. But I decided to let that be chitchat, mostly, though Rasmussen spoke as articulately as he had spoken before. He explained some of the details of ESP-TV and talked about his past experience in sports. All the while, he seemed less nervous than when he had delivered the opening-round presentation to me in Los Angeles less than a month before. It was a beautiful flight over the deserts and massive rock formations, some of which seemed like humongous, misplaced sculpture.

We arrived in Phoenix in the early afternoon and met up with Harold Stuart without a hitch. From there, we headed across the great expanses of sand toward Texas. Berg, Stuart, Rasmussen, and I sat together in the plane's conference area.

My communication strategy for the meeting was that of a kind of straight man. I dislike the term, but it communicates what I wanted to do, namely, prompt the discussion to some of the key things that I knew, or had learned, but let Bill Rasmussen articulate them. I tried to steer the discussion to certain aspects that I thought were important. Knowing the two executives as I did, I tossed out questions that dealt primarily with background, programming and revenues, and satellite technology.

"Bill, did your experience at the University of Connecticut help you understand better the way sports programming works?" I asked, wide-eyed as a child.

"Yes, it puts you on another level. Sports people often want to talk to you—coaches and the like," Rasmussen said.

I wanted to relate to Getty somehow, maybe stroke a little corporate ego, so I segued into a question about Getty's power and influence. I referred to the NCAA.

"With the prospect of Getty Oil's interest, have you found that it's opened doors with the NCAA, relative to programming?"

Rasmussen smiled and said, "Oh, my gosh, I could hardly get through the door before I mentioned Getty. It became much easier." He had been called out of a meeting to come west, so had some fresh takes on future potential with the NCAA.

The two Harolds seemed pleased and offered up a couple of questions about cable and technical matters.

Then I ventured into the issue of advertising: a money pit, which, at the time, seemed deep and dark. Initially, it was hard to see the money flowing in to these untested waters. I had known of one recent bit of encouraging news that way, and because I figured that the question of revenues and revenue streams would come up, why not beat them to it? "How does it look insofar as advertising?" I asked.

"Anheuser-Busch has made a tentative agreement to buy one-eighth of a package of advertising," Rasmussen said, with a gleeful look.

"What's that mean in dollars?" Berg asked.

"It's about $1.3 million," Rasmussen said.

"They're taking a risk," Stuart chimed in.

"They're not committed to pay yet—unless it goes," Rasmussen reminded everyone.

"But it's still a risk."

I couldn't tell if Harold Stuart's words indicated a layer of pessimism on his part. Both Stuart and Berg seemed concerned about the satellite deadline. Rasmussen said, essentially, that even the good name of Getty probably wouldn't buy us any extra time on the deadline with RCA for Satcom 1.

We talked about ideas for the opening launch among other things, and soon the pilot had lowered the flaps and we were drawing closer and closer to the runway at Midland-Odessa Airport. The first installment of the trip had gone satisfactorily. At least no one had ushered me to the back of the plane for a crushingly disappointing salvo of some sort. "Couldn't we do this without him?" "What does he bring?"

We had arranged for two limos, which we found waiting at the airport, ready to take us to a small hotel in downtown Midland. I directed Rasmussen toward the first limo, along with Harold Berg and Harold Stuart, wondering if I was doing the right thing. Perhaps I should be there every moment. What if I was needed to offer a correction or explanation? Though the canned approach—Stu as straight man—that I had taken on the flight had gone reasonably well, I knew it didn't offer much of an opportunity for the Getty executives to get to know Bill Rasmussen on a personal basis, and that was part of the reason for the trip.

I climbed into the other limo with John McCabe and the two wives and watched Bill Rasmussen join the two Harolds in the first limousine. He would have to deal with the amplitude of questions like someone who'd done it many times before.

Thus far, it felt as though we'd played half the game and the score was still tied. This trip would make it or break it. We sped past stretches of cacti at 70 miles per hour, I remember, in a vivid way, the wind outside our limo, a wind tempered by the posh, quilted interior of the vehicle. I felt insular for the moment, but the wind was there, as if the outside world still existed, and that even money, inherent in an expensive limousine, couldn't completely quiet things. Similarly, I wondered if money alone could make ESP-TV a successful entity in the portfolios of Getty. My mind was jumping like this.

Shortly, I focused on Rasmussen and wondered if he had the ability to spearhead the fledgling effort in the longterm. I had, more or less, decided he couldn't. Rasmussen was a promoter, and promoters often did not work well within the corporate ranks. They tended to be impatient men, and although I was impatient, I fit the corporate mold. Where would I get the men or women who would lead ESPN, Rasmussen or not?

After a short trip, maybe 10 or 15 minutes, our limousines pulled up to the hotel and we all got out. Anxiously I mustered up a faultless smile. I got my suitcase and briefcase from the trunk of the limousine and started toward the hotel. At that point I looked over at Harold Berg to see how the ride with Rasmussen had gone. Berg looked at me and flashed me a subtle nod. It was OK. It was approved. I worry too much.

Moments later, I noticed Bill Rasmussen checking in at the front desk. I walked up behind him, grabbed him by the arm, and said, "Bill, congratulations!"

There was no long wait for the corporation to grind slowly to a decision. Instead, the meeting took place and the decision was made. In a sense, the whole approach felt instinctual, to me and perhaps to Harold Berg. I knew that if Berg got the unconditional support of Harold Stuart, the proposal would be accepted, but all the information had to be right. And it had to be orchestrated.

When I congratulated him, Rasmussen's mouth dropped open. The fighting for his idea was, at last, over. After all he had gone through—all the rejections, false starts, letdowns, and setbacks—the idea was going to get a chance, at least, to spread its wings past this small, dusty Texas town, toward the nation, the world, maybe.

As we flew back to Los Angeles the next day, I called my staff at Getty and told them that Harold Berg had given his approval to do the ESPN project. They sounded excited at the news. I also said that we needed to get together for a meeting with Bill Rasmussen as soon as he and I arrived back at headquarters. The next step would be to notify the financial department to get the required paperwork prepared.

Everything seemed to be working, I scribbled out an authorization for Harold Berg's signature. Although I had the authority to advance that amount of money, I wanted to keep everything formal. Soon, Getty Oil cut a check for the first portion of the $10 million originally requested by Rasmussen and sent it off to the King of Prussia, Pennsylvania, offices of K. S. Sweet and Associates. (I would have guessed that K. S. Sweet quickly took back their advances.)

Then came the time for negotiations on Rasmussen's stock and other aspects. I knew they would be tough because of the speculative nature of the deal. I was looking at investing $10 million of Getty Oil money in a venture with no guarantees whatsoever. Every time I thought of the deal, I thought of the other executives that I knew—or didn't know—who had turned down the same opportunity. Among those people who had refused ESP-TV were some good business minds with solid, storied experiences.

I felt determined that no one was going to take that amount of money for an idea that might or might not have merit—or even a modicum of a chance to be successful. The idea, at that time, was a miniature version of what it grew to be, but even at that stage I felt strongly that everyone should share the financial risk. I made it clear going into the negotiations that the Rasmussens were not going to get money out of the transaction until such time as the profits dictated.

As a result, the conditions I set forth were the following: Getty would buy 85 percent of the total outstanding stock of the ESP-TV Company, which was comprised mostly of the Rasmussen family and their associates' stock interests. That meant that Bill Rasmussen and the others retained 15 percent of stock holdings in the company.

But the real condition of us buying ESP-TV, and pledging the $10 million, was that no stock of the minority stockholder group could be sold or transferred—or no dividends extended—until such time as Getty Oil Company had recovered its present or future investment. That was a key point because the sum of $10 million grew to $55 million during our ownership.

I guess I became the heavy in the negotiation. I think Bill Rasmussen is quoted as saying that I changed after the commitment was made. I didn't view it that way. I simply put on another hat. I didn't feel I was going for the jugular vein. ESP-TV had no real value except for what we could make of it: no assets except for Getty money. It needed lots of facilities and equipment before it seemed like anything more than a paper corporation.

I always figured in negotiations that the other person had the right to say no, and Bill Rasmussen certainly did. I guess I was being a good corporate man, trying to make the best deal I could for the investor. Throughout the negotiation, though, which probably lasted no more than an hour, Rasmussen seemed amenable to the decisions that were made.

Valuing what Rasmussen had done, I wanted to see that he received a good salary, so we set up salaries for him and his son, Scott. Bill's, as I recall, was $100,000 per year, and his son's was to be $50,000 a year. Not bad salaries in 1979. In fact, $100,000 was significantly more than the amount midlevel Getty executives made, many of whom had been with the corporation for 20 years or more and had executed many important deals for us. Dan Burke, my number one executive assistant, had served the company for 20 years and was making approximately $75,000 at the time. I will admit that the Rasmussens received no benefits, largely because ESP-TV did not have benefits for some time. But it was a fair starting point for a guy and his son who had an idea—a good one, it turned out, but still an unproven idea—and no money. Furthermore, I figured that future hires would be based on the salary that Bill Rasmussen got, so I couldn't set the bar too high or I'd risk a top-heavy payroll. (Chet Simmons joined ESPN as president at a salary of $225,000 per year; Scotty Connal earned a salary in the high five figures as executive producer.)

I began to reflect more on the future of the new network and the role Bill Rasmussen could reasonably be expected to play in it. I kept coming back to the idea that he was primarily a promoter, the man who, in the chain of events, gets everything started. He is the explosive catalyst. But I soon decided that he was not exactly of the corporate mold—as I had feared. Soon, he began showing up on the covers of magazines, speaking roundly on issues as if he were a celebrity.

It wasn't long before I found myself deep in the miasma of what I used to call "deal separating." Rasmussen had gone around, like a good promoter would, and made a number of tentative agreements with companies, deals that were contingent on ESP-TV's finding financial backing. For six months or more, I took calls from companies that had found out ESP-TV was a go and wanted us to buy this or that, as sanctioned by Rasmussen. Of course, he had no authority to speak for Getty Oil, which I tried to tell most of them. In many cases, we needed the product or service the companies represented, and Rasmussen knew how to find the quality companies, but I found it, nonetheless, confounding. It seemed that it took me at least six months, from the time we came on board in February to the time ESP-TV launched in September, to cut through those preagreements, tentative or speculative as they might have been.

I did the deals, or undid them, or got our people to look closely at them. One company, Compact Video of Burbank, experts in mobile truck units and broadcast centers, had designed a broadcast center on spec, and we followed through on a lot that had been projected by them and Rasmussen. "Three to five mobile units—$2 million each."

The toughest deal separation was when I had to talk Marty Pasetta out of the million dollars he'd been offered by Rasmussen to produce the opening launch show. That was uncomfortable for me, to say the least, because Pasetta was a man who had moved to the top of his profession, a man who had directed such legendary galas as the Academy Awards, and now I had to tell him where we at ESPN stood financially. Luckily, he understood. I will be forever grateful to Pasetta for what was more than a small gesture. It was the 1970's equivalent of the lottery, and ESPN owes an eternal debt (in thanks) to Marty Pasetta. In a lawsuit, even in the slightly less litigious times of yesteryear, he might well have won.

Then I realized something—the $10 million would be severely depleted in about three months, partly due to Rasmussen's prior agreements, which, while necessary for him initially, were not known at the time of our deal. After about three weeks, I began thinking, "Oh, shit," as I began to have to think about another $10 million. Where would it stop? The bleeding had just started, and I knew somehow it would not stop soon—if at all.

Along the way and shortly before the launch in 1979, it was determined that Bill Rasmussen's services would no longer be required. The company was in an operating mode with President Chet Simmons exerting total direction of management and operations. Simmons and his staff could handle the press. After I named Rasmussen chairman to vacate the president's position for Simmons, the relationship between the two was strained and became increasingly disruptive to the organization.

We began to get inquiries from a bank, Ted Turner's company, and others who said they'd been offered stock in ESPN by Bill Rasmussen. They planned to pay for the stock, but said they would like to have the stock released and assigned to them. We began to realize that Bill Rasmussen was attempting to sell stock he did not, in effect, own. It was locked up under our agreement. We courteously told the inquiring parties about the stock lock-up agreement, and they did not call again. We finally wrote up a form letter to respond to questions about the availability of Rasmussen's stock, to say that the stock in the new network could not be assigned.

Later, after ABC bought Getty's 85 percent of ESPN, the shares went to Rasmussen. Corporations do not like minority stockholders. As a consequence, ABC lawyers negotiated for the remaining 15 percent of stock from him for a sum of $6 million. Rasmussen held the low position in terms of negotiations, and he must have realized that ABC didn't really need to give him anything and could continue the lock-up provisions. Getty and ABC had invested so much money by then that the lock-up clause I negotiated—which would transfer to ABC as part of the sale— would have required that several hundred million dollars in profit come back to the original investors before Rasmussen could collect anything by selling his stock.

Unfortunately for Bill Rasmussen, he had apparently assigned a lot of his stock away to family members, like his brother Don, who spearheaded a family effort at raising early money to support the venture. Don is owed a significant place in ESPN's history, but he and Rasmussen are currently on the outs over the final disposition of money from the family's and the original partners' investment. And Rasmussen is not too anxious to share his top billing for ESPN with anyone. Finally, by the time Bill Rasmussen had settled with those who had purchased stock out of the ABC proceeds, he was left with only about $1.2 million.

Being the optimist that I am, I had decided that with the launch of ESPN, all kinds of sponsors would flood to us and begin to sign on. "Prospects are good," I planned to announce to everybody I ran across in the Getty hallways. But actual revenues were enough to harden the heart of the bravest investor. Even a $50,000 spec agreement here or there seemed like $1 million, but I wasn't optimistic enough to truly believe it was. I was bouncing off the walls, which was treacherous, as my office walls were mostly made of glass and I was 18 stories up.

I will repeat what I've said so often, and which I think bears repeating: if I'd have told all the bad news I knew, Getty would have been out of ESPN after the first two weeks!

I'm not going to defend my relationship with Bill Rasmussen. I am going to say that if he truly was sympathetic about my position in regard to the deal for ESPN, he might have softened some of the statements he has made in publications. If he had known the tremendous pressure I was under during those times, I think he might not have said some things at all.

The same applies to Chet Simmons. Some of my ideas might not have been very good, but to call me "a jock sniffer" after some of the contributions I made because of past relationships of myself and Getty Oil seems wrongly directed. For example, early on I negotiated with Steve Garvey for public relations work. The Hall of Fame baseball player and former Dodgers great agreed to represent ESPN and do seven public relations events at conventions, as well as to travel to Cincinnati for the Davis Cup, for a nominal sum. We provided him with a leased red Corvette for a year and gave him a personalized license plate: ESPN#1. Further, I got the distinguished actor John Forsythe to do a major segment of the opening launch show at no charge. These were examples of ways in which I thought I could contribute a little extra to the effort. Damn me for something else, dammit!

Over time, I think the people at Getty did appreciate some of the deals I pulled off in their various configurations, while I think most others—including many at ESPN—did not. While the Getty people didn't know the amount of money I was saving them, they did have a sense that I was conscious of the purse strings and trying to find innovative ways to get the word about ESPN out to the public. I always figured that anyone could go and pay someone half a million to do something for them. It took a little more guile and a touch of persuasion to get big people to do mundane, even boring things, for little or no pay.

By now, the ESPN operation was underway, Getty revenues from it's core business had begun, around 1980, to head down. Still, for whatever reason, Getty was only looking for highlights. That was too fitting, perhaps, in a world of sports satellite television, where highlights were everything—as evidenced by the success of *SportsCenter* and other shows. Soon, ESPN was only a reporting item, which was good and bad. Now reduced to dollars and cents, there were fewer ways to mask the financial situation I had engendered. I could offer reasons, but I had promised a lot.

After the deal, I thought things would begin to ease; however, I was still spending 120 percent of my time on ESPN, trying to sandwich my many other duties into days that began way too early. To this day I am an early riser. I can't stop it, though I wish I could. That came about, largely and dramatically, when ESPN came into my life. I had to get up early in the morning to have conversations with the ESPN folks in Connecticut or New York. When the East Coast day started, it was 6:00 A.M. on the West Coast, and at that time, ESPN people had begun their rounds of meetings and discussions. If I were to speak with someone there, I needed to catch that person then, within that window of opportunity. If I waited until I got to the office at Getty, I would miss the people at ESPN because by then people went to lunch. After that, I lost time because I headed off to lunch. (There were no cell phones in those days, which might have helped, or cursed, the effort.) If I missed the time frame between 5:00 and 6:30 in the morning, important things didn't get said or implemented. I know that is a common problem for people who operate on both coasts, but I think of it often now when I try to force my old and tired body to resist the long habit of waking early.

In my deepest self, I consider myself an optimist. I think I am that way because I don't like to be any other way. I want to make things work, whether it's a toy at Christmas or a $10 million deal. That means sometimes I have to make things work temporarily until they gain root, like a newly planted tree, and proceed on their own.

One has to be an optimist to have the kind of fears I have sometimes— not the typical, deep fears that make everything seem improbable, but those where a possible and hoped-for outcome sits engagingly close, teasing you, as in a game of golf when the ball sits on the edge of the critical 18th hole, waiting for a nudge. When the shot pulled up way short, it was not so bad. Now, though, the ball is tottering and you almost pray for a wind gust to knock it in. Ethics matters. You won't cheat, though tempted.

Sometimes, though, being an optimist creates mountains beyond our imaginings—the opportunity now created by that part of yourself which won't let you say no. Then you discover that you can't get there, the terrain's too steep, the mountain should have been smaller. If you get there, you can be an optimist again.

But there's always a mountain. Unfortunately, I got to a point in my career where the mountains lined up successively like a huge range, some so high I couldn't see the tops of them in the separation of fog. I'd climb one and then, given the type-A personality that I have, set my sights on one a little higher. Pretty soon, I would run out of fingernails, worn out by clawing up that mountain. The idea of surpassing oneself, however, is a real one, at least as real and true as a metaphor. That idea of climbing the mountain controlled my life, to some extent, after the success of ESPN. But where were the other mountains—in Bristol or anywhere? Where does one go from there? Can one always keep going up? First, however, I had to worry how this paper company of ESPN was going to shed its infant status to become a corporation with real assets, talented people, a quality product, and developing markets.

CHAPTER 10

WHERE THE HELL IS BRISTOL, CONNECTICUT?

I f there were a top ten for questions when we started ESPN, the question of ESPN's location probably would have ranked high—possibly number one or two.

"It's right near Hartford," I'd answer.

"No, it isn't in England," I answered a few times. "Actually, there is one in England, but it's not ours."

Bristol, Connecticut, a small community about 16 miles from Hartford, seemed an unlikely location to start what would become an enormous media operation such as ESPN, but it also made sense—as in dollars and cents. Bill Rasmussen had already obtained an option on four sections of land close to the city of Bristol with favorable terms and incentives by city officials. Before we had met, he had purchased a little more than 25 percent of the land for $18,000. After the launch, and over the next three years, the deal for the remaining land in the parcel was finalized.

I figured that the decision for the network to be in Bristol, which the fates seemed to have taken away from me, wasn't inherently good or inherently bad. I simply didn't know. I was too busy to really consider it. Why not go with it? After all, where else could one find a place with room to grow and a corps of supportive public officials that was conveniently close to New York? At the time, I believe, New York rented for $100 per square foot, and considering the number of square feet we needed, I thought, "We'll make it work." Besides, the vistas I envisioned had little to do with skylines, unless they involved telecommunications technology.

Still, others continued to ask, "Why not Denver?" At the very time we were settling on Bristol, we were told frequently that, in Denver, the proximity to a number of other cable-related operations would be invaluable, and that the satellites used for cable television were located directly above Denver. We didn't know enough at the time to know if it mattered. Ignorance can be, if not bliss, valuable. Bristol would remain headquarters for ESPN for the foreseeable future, and for certain until revenues and profits dictated otherwise.

When we started, we had two satellite dishes, concave masterworks I might have mistaken for small, above-ground swimming pools before the ESPN venture. Today, the ESPN campus is so laden with satellite dishes, more than 27, that a visitor from outer space who didn't understand the signals might think the dishes had sent out a mating call and their kind had come from all over the universe.

After a number of clients and employees had wended their way through the small towns on the way to Bristol, we began to realize that location had an inherent weakness: while only two hours from New York City, the trip was energy-sapping. The talent that needed to arrive fresh wasn't always fresh; the business meetings with outsiders that otherwise might be brief, were often compromised by the lengthy two-way commute. Still, because of the strains on capital, we couldn't enjoy the luxury of considering other options. In the early days, ESPN, although on the air, was still under construction, with no single office to serve as a meeting place for the architect or construction executive, potential sponsor or ESPN sales representative. Instead, meetings frequently took place at the nearby Farmington Inn, a comfortable, modest-sized motel that we literally took over in mid-1979 until the broadcast center was completed and the executives and senior staff had relocated their families to permanent residences. Most meetings were held in Chet Simmons' room, which, because it was his office as well as his living quarters, was larger than the standard rooms.

The shortening intervals between important meetings, especially with advertising and cable folks, caused us to rethink our Bristol location. At that point, management determined that a New York City presence was mandatory if we were to maintain timely and efficient relationships with the industry cable, sales, and advertising representatives. Revenue reports, along with other indicators, soon showed us that being close to key players mattered. Our offices on Lexington Avenue, though not lavish, allowed our administrative and legal staffs to minimize the commute to Bristol, and the immediate benefits of this decision were quickly realized.

The commute, inevitable for some, meant that the company had to spend a lot of money on hotels in New York. To partially minimize these costs, we decided to lease a two-bedroom apartment on 57th Street in New York City, complete with a doorman. The lease was approximately $2,000 each month and provided a nice, clean, economical place where executives and others could stay. I and other Getty executives would stay there often on the way to or from Bristol, but as ESPN grew, the need for some of us to spend time in Bristol lessened.

Just before ESPN was launched, few people outside the industry knew how satellite-delivered cable television really worked. Certainly, not all of the members of the board at Getty Oil, except for those few to whom I had spoken in depth, comprehended the magnitude of the investment they had approved. To better inform our people about what I was trying to achieve, I recommended that the board hold its July 1980 board of directors meeting in Bristol. I was convinced that if I could make a proper show of the fledgling operation, it would help me in future negotiations with our directors. The recommendation was accepted, and the board members flew into Hartford, Connecticut. They were met by ESPN personnel and driven to the headquarters and broadcast center. No mahogany graced the facilities, no deep, plush carpets dulled the sounds of the rooms. In fact, the whole ESPN facility, with its makeshift trailers and half-finished buildings fairly clanged.

That evening, ESPN president Chet Simmons and his wife, Harriet, hosted a gathering in their home for the directors and selected ESPN management. In the days prior to the director's visit, Simmons and I reviewed the strategy for this meeting and tour. Plain and simple, it was to impress the directors with ESPN's progress in the few short months since the launch and to express our optimism that its potential was enormous. The meeting was a success because each person had a factual and honest story to relate.

As the evening progressed, I was comforted to notice that executives from both companies were chatting about matters of common interest. Lawyers talking with lawyers. Banker board members like Chauncey Medberry, chairman of Bank of America; Frederick Larkin, chairman of Security Pacific National Bank; and Willard Boothby, chairman of Blythe Eastman Dillon chatted with ESPN financial executives. All seemed to be enjoying their contact with these newcomers and veterans of the television industry. Harold Berg, the chief executive of Getty was there too, and he had been a supporter of the ESPN investment from the beginning. Chet Simmons, the chief executive of ESPN, seemed pleased because he could see that the visitors were warming to his staff. Then I noticed a happy phenomenon: the ESPN employees, including Scotty Connal, our brilliant executive director, had struck up excited conversations with members of the board. In fact, I could hear animated sports talk all around the room.

"Did you ever meet Davey Johnson of the New York Mets?"

"I played a little baseball in high school."

"Who's going to win the Masters this year?"

Conversation replaced wariness. The sports varied, but the excitement was the same. I was witnessing what I had so strongly felt to be true, that sports are a kind of universal language, and here I was watching it creep into the world of business.

I couldn't have been more pleased. Although there were queries and concerns about the slow progress of ESPN's revenues and greater need for capital, I could sense that the mood in the room would make future budget requests far more palatable. To take advantage of this very successful evening, I asked Harold Berg if I might make a brief presentation about ESPN's recent accomplishments and the optimism that prevailed. He, too, thought the directors had enjoyed the evening and seemed very pleased with what he had seen and heard.

The next morning, the sky outside was a heaven of blue glass as far as I could see. As I dressed, I began to feel uncomfortable in this world of cable. I felt foreign there, and Bristol, lovely as it was, did not seem like my home court. Finally, there was too much that I didn't know about the industry. And unfortunately, I knew the board and its ability to save the tough questions for last too well. I had to muster my energies.

I reasoned, however, that I hadn't really heard anyone say anything negative at the meeting the night before, which I found enormously pleasing. Now I felt that unless I could instill in the board members the importance of equipment and facilities and the uniqueness of the broadcast industry, I was less than successful. What if they hated the business? I knew we needed another broadcast van and soon, and that the price tag on that could run to $2 million.

As I considered the remarks I would make, I flashed back to Walter O'Malley, chairman of the Los Angeles Dodgers, whom I thought of often in those days. He was an inspiration—a clever, crazy, wonderful inspiration. I had met O'Malley when George Getty and his first wife, Gloria, divorced and sold their home in the prominent Hancock Park area of Los Angeles. I handled the transaction, and the buyer was none other than Walter O'Malley, who had recently moved his Dodgers from Brooklyn to Los Angeles. Since that time, we had become friends. O'Malley was a great teaser and maybe reminded me of my own propensity to joke and tease. Still, he was genuine and had genuine affection for his friends—even if he was roasting them.

I was to introduce him and several of the Los Angeles Dodgers, including manager Walter Alston, at the Father-Son Banquet at the Los Angeles Club, a private organization on the top floor of the Getty building. I suddenly felt the urgent call of the urinal and rushed to the rest room. Upon returning, I looked around for the notes I'd written for my introductions. Finally, unable to find them, I began to panic. Then I looked over and across the table and saw something on the far edges, a bird's nest of torn and ripped paper: my precious notes. Who was the joker? Then I looked at O'Malley, who was sitting there smoking a Cuban cigar with a cherubic smile broadening on his face. "Let's see how good you are," he said, so amused he might have fallen out of his chair had he not fit in it so tightly. That night I made it through, and have made it many nights since.

I could make it through this presentation to the board of directors.

When the zero hour approached, an idea that later would become an oft-quoted piece of brilliance rushed to mind. Even though I didn't know how it would turn out, I felt I had no choice but to cajole them out of more money to protect their investment. I had been at enough board meetings to know how these conservative bankers and oil men worked. They would just flip through budget proposals, the cost of oil wells, approving incredible amounts of money to keep the drilling alive on a potential well site. Yet this ESPN investment drew great attention and interest in every detail. I might not be able to control spiraling costs. I would never know everything I needed to know about the always-changing broadcast cable sports industry. But the more I heard the naysayers at network television, the more I trusted—believed intuitively—that eventually this ESPN investment would be a gusher.

That day I commenced my remarks with oil patch vernacular: "Gentlemen, in early 1979, when I first proposed the ESPN project as a possible investment for the Getty Oil Company, I told you our initial exploration investigations showed that the geological surveys and seismic studies showed that we had discovered a reservoir worth tapping." As I carefully delivered each word to build drama, I felt my confidence rise, even as I set them up. It almost sounded like the beginning of a resignation speech, or at least signs that I might finally tell them the truth about what they had all expected: that I had been wrong from the beginning. Their investment commitment of nearly $50 million by this time was a waste.

"I felt it would be a viable venture." Having said that, I would know momentarily if my dream would stay alive. If only I could get them to laugh! I tried to smile in a way that wouldn't betray my confidence in what I was about to say. "When you authorized the capital necessary to start this business, I told you our mission was to find a reservoir. Today, I am pleased to tell you that the reservoir has been discovered." I thought I could see lust in their eyes. They were now hanging on every word.

"However . . ." I paused. I could feel the stares and hear the silence. "Gentlemen, not only has the reservoir been discovered, it is much, much bigger than I originally envisioned, it is much, much deeper, and I need more drill pipe to reach the objective." The room, full of men who had been seduced by the promise of early riches, erupted into laughter. It had been a slam dunk presentation, one that people still remember as one of those moments in which legends are made. ESPN's budget requests for the next year were passed, even as the board of directors casually flipped through the details.

After the board meeting, we toured the facilities: the primitive broadcast center control room with its flashing lights and monitors illustrating games and events from all over the world, and the satellite control room, which showed the picture being uplinked to Satcom 1, 23,500 miles away, and returned to satellite receivers in one-fifth of a second. Then we took in the view of the proliferation of Earth stations covering the grounds outside the broadcast center, pointing in every direction to send and receive signals from anywhere in the world. After a tour of the remote mobile broadcast vans, we were taken to the airport and back home to the West Coast.

I watched, keen-eyed for the feared horizon of scowls, but only observed a couple of smiles that I thought might have come more from satiation or courtesy than from satisfaction with the concept. I couldn't know the outcome. I was selling for the future, which is not always the easiest thing to do. In those days, not now as an older man, I tended to think of the future, which was perhaps a weakness sometimes. But in that situation, I was thinking hard of the present.

Later on, I learned that the visit to Bristol, which many described as "NBC North" because of the many employees hired away from that network in the early days, had pushed aside many of the earlier concerns the board might have had. In the future, when I talked about the need for more Earth stations and other capital requirements, members' faces showed recognition, and they approved the requests. The trip to Bristol had given the members of the board a visual picture of things. It was as if we were drilling for another oil well that all had seen occur. Regardless of where the board was physically, ESPN was in their minds. It was just another oil well.

Beano Cook, retired ESPN analyst, once said, "What Bogart and Bergman did for Casablanca, ESPN has done for Bristol." I am proud of our relationship with Bristol, and it's probably fortuitous that the corporation still sits there today, especially with the increasing rental rates in the city. The little town that helped build ESPN was, in turn, built by ESPN. Today the population has increased to sixty thousand.

Sal Marchiano, a former boxing analyst, became irritated and left his job at ESPN. In parting, he said, "There's no better view of Bristol than from my rearview mirror." I thought it funny, but untrue. Thank you, Bristol, for your early—and continuing—support.

CHAPTER 11

LIGHTS! CAMERA! ACTION?

The ESPN start date sat on the horizon of my mind, bold as a satellite: September 7, 1979. Whether it was fear of failure or a desire to keep busy that stimulated the promotional side of my personality, I don't know, but I decided that I needed to develop some sort of communication that would help draw attention to this new and precarious venture of an all-sports television network.

I contacted a friend, Bunker Jenkins, a veteran comedy writer with *Candid Camera*. Anxious to put his new video camera to work, he agreed to meet me at the fabled Santa Anita race course. I recall the bright, sun-drenched track and how it seemed as if the light would shine exclusively on my companions and me that day. As we found our box at the track, I scanned the panoply of celebrities, many of whom I had known at least casually during the days I owned my own racehorses or managed George Getty's. There must have been some jokes about the money I'd frittered away in my pursuit of the perfect thoroughbred.

I shook hands with the men in the box, feeling suddenly like the king of central casting. There before me, dapper in seersucker suits, broad hats, casual shirts, and trousers, lounged comedian Milton Berle, actor and dancer Fred Astaire, Henry Slate (from the Slate Brothers comedy act), and comedian George Jessel, who was wearing his trademark distinctive admiral's outfit befitting of all those postal jokes.

I told them what ESPN was going to be. Immediately, I felt anything but a guarded celebrity reaction. When I asked them if I could videotape them and their responses and send them back to ESPN for promotion, they all smiled as if it were a gentle enough folly.

Berle said, "I'll do it," and flashed those famous teeth. The camera rolled, and he looked at the lens and spoke: "Gee, this is going to be fantastic. I stay up all night drinking and screwing. Now I'll be able to stay in bed and watch sports." He paused and said, "What was that network again?" I had to pinch myself when he finished. Imagine, a testimonial for a new television network from none other than "Mr. Television" himself, Milton Berle.

Bunker flanked over next to Fred Astaire for his testimonial, aimed, and started to shoot. In his urbane way, Astaire spoke and expressed interest in whether this new network would telecast horse racing. From the next box over, Walter Matthau joined in, "Yeah, but can you gamble on it?"

Next came comedian George Jessel, who seemed truly excited about the prospect, more so than the other ad-libbers. "It's just wonderful," he said. "Television has been my life. I'm just anxious for everything to get on television." (I thought that was the understatement of the year.)

Bunker, a man who had rigged up plenty of jokes and surprises, delighted in the spontaneity of the exchanges. But I didn't know what our new president Chet Simmons would say about them when I sent off an edited version the next day. I thought he would like it or, at the very least, appreciate that I had gotten a lot of big names on our side—a big bang for no bucks. And so what if it was funky or goofy? After all, I reasoned, there was nothing expected of ESPN at that time. If it wasn't done top-grade with expensive equipment and lots of people all around, so what? I figured that this wasn't the mindset of cable, especially considering what I had seen to that point. Besides, we had major stars goofing around in their element, and it was funny.

Unfortunately, Chet Simmons didn't find the testimonials the least bit in sync with his working ideas of promotion. Already stressed about the early start date, he shot back: "This is an incredible piece of garbage, and it isn't funny." I knew then that my future didn't rest in producing commercials or promos—but I certainly hoped it rested with a sports network—and, still, I did have one more promotion I had to try.

I had made up my mind that I was going to fashion yet another celebrity piece. I contacted my friend, John Forsythe, the actor whose distinctive, dulcet voice communicated assignments to Charlie's angels in the television show by the same name. Forsythe and I once had owned a racehorse together, a thoroughbred named Bold Mamselle. He seemed pleased to hear from me, and after I explained the plan, he quickly agreed to help. I asked him to meet me early in the morning at Santa Anita, the location of my previous videotape failure. Santa Anita was one of my favorite racetracks. A few miles down the road from Pasadena in Arcadia, the historic and storied track sits at the base of the San Gabriel Mountains. Affirmed began his 1978 Triple Crown run here. And in 1987, Laffit Pincay won a record seven races on March 14.

A large ESPN production van met us there in the parking lot, where we proceeded to tape. Later, I reminded Forsythe of the experience: "You remember, don't you, John? You did it in the parking lot." And he said with a grin, "I've never done it in a parking lot."

During the taping, Forsythe was wonderful, generous, urbane, dignified—his usual self. I thought this surely would be an image that ESPN could front successfully. No matter what Simmons said, I intended to push for its use. When we finished the taping, which Forsythe successfully ad-libbed in less than an hour, I felt confident. It was all from scratch. It had to work. I hated to think of wasting this important man's time if Simmons would not use the footage.

The shot opened with Forsythe polishing the fender of a huge tractor-trailer television truck. He turned to the camera and spoke as effortlessly as only he can: "Hi! This vehicle is just what it appears to be, a truck. But it is a most unusual truck." He explained that the truck was a studio with wheels and, in explaining its cost in the neighborhood of $2 million, he added, "For a small convoy, that's quite a neighborhood." Even for a regular on the famous *Dallas* television series, price was an object.

Forsythe moved easily around the van, explaining it as a kind of growth symbol of cable before he gave a brief history of the cable field. Much of our focus during the taping in Santa Anita—and later in Bristol for the other segments of the first show—was to explain this new technology. Cable started as a way to reach areas that were inaccessible, Forsythe explained, and then he discussed how cable was primarily used to improve reception and then programming. He referred to ESPN as "the most exciting supplier in cable television." Then he listed a number of sports, and said, "Just about every sport you can think of—indoors or outdoors. So if you're a sports nut like I am, it'll be like having seven Sundays in every week."

At the time of the videotaping, Forsythe had given away no hint of his true attitude about the project. He later told me, "I had no idea that it was going to be a success. I was doing whatever I did off the cuff, and I was doing it because I had a good friend. Frankly, I thought it was the dumbest thing I'd ever heard of."

Luckily, Forsythe's personal feelings didn't show through his acting performance. And happily, I didn't have to wait long for Chet Simmons, back at headquarters, to return my call and agree with me about the merits of using the Forsythe tape to promote our new endeavor. ESPN featured John Forsythe for the opening day ceremony.

I was concerned about the ESPN launch for many reasons, not the least of which was the force of personalities that seemed to be colliding like wayward objects in orbit. Chet Simmons opposed Bill Rasmussen on a September start date for the new network, and Simmons' arrival in Bristol fueled continuing tension with Bill and Scott Rasmussen. Simmons resented that he had to share a 10' x 12' office with the two men. He also hated the fact that the Rasmussens were driving Cadillacs paid for by ESPN. Such a perk seemed bad enough in a cash-strapped company for an older person, but for young 23-year-old Scott, it seemed preposterous. Simmons said that if he'd had Scott for a son, he'd have "put him in a Toyota—and he'd pay for it."

The Rasmussens attracted the attention of the press and began talking about ESPN's future plans. I thought they were, in a sense, creatures of the press, and that Simmons and I clearly needed to rein them in. If they stopped talking so much, I reasoned, the press might back away. But the Rasmussens seemed to react as if it were jealousy, which was anything but the case. At the time, ESPN was the subsidiary of a public company, with real stockholders, which meant it had to meet certain legal requirements. It was no longer the province of several individuals with an idea. What would happen to the company if a free-speaking, big-dreaming Rasmussen announced some grandiose future plans, and Getty stock bolted up in value? In such a case, an individual, even with a corporate title, can't go out and say anything he or she wants. The lawyers were serious when they reminded me of the implications of speaking out of turn. When I read in the newspapers that the founder of ESPN, Bill Rasmussen, planned this or that event, it really rankled me. Rasmussen maintained that the media was responsible for the attention and that it was not self-promotion. It did begin to seem as though the magazines had taken to quoting Bill and Scott Rasmussen in the great American tradition, as if the two men were really underdogs in a great battle. This struck me as disingenuous because I thought of all of us as underdogs—*big* underdogs.

Soon, *Adweek* declared Bill Rasmussen "one of the 12 biggest headline-makers of the year." *The New York Times* and *Connecticut Magazine* weighed the importance of the Rasmussens and elevated them. In fact, in mid-August, *Connecticut Magazine* featured Bill Rasmussen on the cover with the headline, "Why are ABC, CBS, and NBC afraid of this man?" Indeed, he was important, but he was but one cog in a new wheel, and he had to learn his position there—soon.

The launch of the ESPN idea was to be September 7, 1979. On September 6, I flew from Los Angeles to New York, then drove to Bristol, where I spent the night. The next morning, I got up tired, excited, and trying to remind my rational half that there were no reasons to feel apprehensive.

I ate a quick breakfast and went to ESPN headquarters, where I watched and waited. As the morning of the launch wore on, I felt more engaged and, yes, more nervous. I felt like a track athlete waiting to run in the last event of the day. I was cheering the others on. Who would be left to cheer me on after this day had passed? Even a successful launch didn't guarantee a complete success. I wanted to imagine that everything would go perfectly, but it couldn't and wouldn't. Then I heard in the late afternoon that one of the tractors hauling equipment for the unfinished broadcast center had accidentally rammed into a mobile unit, badly shaking up the vehicle.

We were also told the wiring had some "bugs." Would the signal make it to the remote truck so that it could get relayed to the satellite? The "bugs" descended in greater numbers. All I could think of was winged and flying things, including the image of dead birds evoked by a mayoral incumbent who, during an election year, said that radiation from our Earth stations would kill the birds of Bristol. We had brought in an engineer-consultant who successfully countered those charges. Now, time was running close to launch, and we wouldn't bring in any miracle workers to solve our problems. Then, too, the place was filled with flies, smacking against the windows like they wanted to get out. While our technicians and engineers scurried to solve the metaphoric "bugs," I swatted at a few of the other kind.

Another problem had arisen earlier when Bill Rasmussen agreed to pay Marty Pasetta, known for high-profile events like the Grammy Awards, $1 million to direct the launch broadcast of ESPN. When I learned of the offer, I was furious, as was Chet Simmons. We could scarcely cover the costs for basic crew, and here we were tossing money away. I met with Pasetta at the Bistro Garden in Los Angeles. I said, "Marty, here's where we are. We cannot possibly have an opening show like Bill envisions. We don't know who the subscribers are. We might go on the air with two people watching." I paused for a while, hoping Pasetta would see it my way. "You know, I hope you understand our position. I have to ask you if you'd be so kind to forego the agreement with Rasmussen—and move on." Pasetta graciously bowed out. Bill Creasy, a friend of Chet Simmons' from NBC, had been working as a programming executive at ESPN. With his background as a former network producer, Creasy was assigned the job of producing the opening show.

The actual starting time of 7:00 P.M. EST was growing close, and still, painters were painting, engineers engineering, carpenters carpentering, and bulldozers dozing mounds of earth around outside. It was chaos, plainly, and tempers and their attendant expletives began to fly. The studio was anything but finished. Gaping holes in its foundation attested to the vulnerability of things. The studio smelled noxiously of fresh paint, and we were all dodging wet sets and walls. Creasy was trying to figure out the order of interviews done with Bill Rasmussen and me. The script for the opening show was, in fact, easily revised and, luckily, Creasy was a steadying presence.

Wrapped up in what was going on that day was a variety of people, including Bill Rasmussen and his wife, Scott Rasmussen, and several advertising folks from D'Arcy McManus, the advertising agency representing Budweiser, our only serious client. Budweiser had signed for an advertisement package that gave them exclusive rights to beer advertising.

Some moments in the day's preparations took on a party atmosphere, and at other times I reflected on the deep sense of what was at stake, although I tried to downplay the importance. In other situations, I likely would have phoned the people at Getty Oil Company to inform them, but I decided against it. It was better to stay on the periphery. Besides, in the culture of Getty, not many people had shown a lot of interest because, as with any far-fetched proposal, if it ever went south, they didn't want to be associated with it. And, personally, I preferred not to drag any more of my friends or colleagues in—or, if they were already in, draw them in yet deeper.

George Grande, who went on to become the distinguished play-by-play man for the Cincinnati Reds, moved into position on the set of *SportsCenter* for the launch. His boyish good looks were more like a movie idol's than a typical sports anchor's. His counterpart that day on *Sports-Center*, Lee Leonard, a cagey and older broadcast veteran, slowly took his place in a chair on the side of the main set. He faced forward, as if to set himself in the box like a big hitter. The two men bantering on the control room monitor looked professional, which I thought was important, even in their garish "school colors"—dressed as they were in the orange blazers of Getty Oil. Despite any potential screw-ups they might confront in their ad-libbing, they seemed to have the right mix of youth and age that advertisers had to embrace. I tried to keep myself distracted from my anxiety by looking over at the Anheuser-Busch representatives in an attempt to read their thoughts, but I couldn't really. Everything was unfolding so fast.

A youthful floor director stepped forward and waved many of our visitors out of the broadcast facility. I watched several turn toward me, as if I could give the OK for them to stay. Sadly, I could only watch.

Suddenly, the countdown began for the show: "Three, two, one. Cue the talent!"

The previously prepared opening for the launch show was a fade-in of a picture of a cheering crowd, which cut to an interior shot of kids with long-haired seventies looks in a high school gymnasium somewhere, which went next to a wide shot of a stadium with a delirium of balloons flying, and then back to my favorite shot of all—a wide-angle shot of the clouds, which I thought at the time, and I think now, seemed as though we were introducing the Reverend Billy Graham's Crusade, not a sports show. The camera zoomed back to reveal the sun in the clouds and the title ESPN superimposed over what looked like a red stoplight behind a magnifying glass. Lee Leonard was speaking in his voice-over, as eloquent as the sun and clouds: "Beyond that blue horizon is a limitless world of sports and, right now, you're standing on the edge of tomorrow."

I was paralyzed in the control room, watching the show unfold. I couldn't believe it was happening.

"This is where all the sports action is as of right now," Leonard said. Everything was orange, and Leonard's jacket faded into the set—as if he had planned to hide. The set featured line drawings of several athletes at play, including a woman playing tennis whose leg appeared in the frame of Leonard's shot some of the time. Only her white tennis outfit was painted in, which got lost, somehow, in the picture, so it looked more like a dove's broken wing.

The *SportsCenter* set stretched across the studio, as long and high as a wall at a country speedway, or the segment of some left-field fence in a minor-league baseball stadium. It was as long as the sports venues that would soon be enumerated and re-enumerated: motor cross, volleyball, swimming, diving, golf, football, baseball, rowing, motorcycle speedways, rugby, basketball, tennis—to name a few, all appearing thanks to the Earth stations or, as Lee Leonard referred to them, "the H. G. Wells invaders of the quiet countryside."

Executive Producer Scotty Connal reasoned that the production would go without the teleprompter—that infamous electric cue card for the talent. His reasoning was that the show would require mostly ad-libbing, and it soon became clear from several of the comments that both Leonard and Grande were having to ad-lib. For example, Leonard said that everybody knew softball as a sport and explained, "We all play it on Sunday when we drink a little beer." Later in the telecast, the conversation between Leonard and Grande turned to Ann Meyers, who had just been signed by the Indiana Pacers of the NBA. Grande said that he considered it a promotional coupe, though he thought because of her 5'9" frame, she wouldn't play in the NBA. Then Lee Leonard, in a sympathetic voice, said, "It's a shame, she is a great athlete. But when you compare her to the dinosaurs that play in the NBA, I would really fear for her life if she were out on the floor with a Bob Lanier or somebody like that." Happily, though, the broadcast discussed the importance of women's sports. Next, Leonard suggested that maybe the audience would "see a woman in the National League or the National Football League or the National Basketball Association."

Chet Simmons, the ESPN president, was beamed up like a reluctant guest, looking less than presidential, sitting as he was in a room full of wooden crates, uncomfortably straddling one, looking almost like a conductor caught hiding from the robbers in the mail car of a midnight train movie. How he ended up in that room is a matter of conjecture—it must have been the only space available at the time for taping—but if someone had ever wanted to make Simmons look small and unimportant, that someone would have chosen just such a location. The camera zoomed in past the white hardhat and settled on Simmons' face, and the bank of monitors in the background suited the distinguished sports journalist. Unfortunately, Simmons referred to ESPN having the necessary "toys," a word that seemed so uncharacteristic of the serious—even hyper-serious—professional.

I had agreed to represent Getty with a brief presentation for the opening show. As my moment in the sun approached, I was feeling good—jovial. However, I did get serious as Leonard introduced me. He began by speaking of "the technological miracle that makes ESPN's around-the-clock sports coverage possible. Now . . . none of it could happen without the basic dollars to finance it. Stuart W. Evey, vice president of Getty Oil Company, which has committed millions of dollars to ESPN this year." The mention of the high-stakes money sobered me—as did the thought of our installed equipment. Would the tape work? I rationalized: I could make a mistake—I was on tape!

The technician then counted down, and the new Sony one-inch video-tape began to spin past its countdown leader. I stood, anticipating my 20 seconds of television glory. The picture set like a sunset on the monitor, and I watched myself walk into the frame, as I had done not three hours before. Then I quickly shook hands with the person who had escorted me out—someone I hardly recognized, but actually was Bill Rasmussen—and who proceeded to exit the scene quickly. Funky staging, yes, but things were going along OK—so far. Then I spoke, and when I did, I sounded as if I were trying extremely hard to evince the same speech rhythms as my childhood idol, Edward R. Murrow, to whom I had listened during those historic World War II broadcasts: "I want to express how pleased we are to be involved with ESPN. We look forward to playing a major role in the growth and development in this exciting new industry. Now, in Los Angeles, a good friend of the cable industry, and a great friend of Getty Oil Company, Mr. John Forsythe."

The audio dropped out once or twice for a second or two, which had happened in several other instances during the broadcast, but I had done my portion, and I stood back, confident that Forsythe would be convincing and serve as an important symbolic presence, a personality who could somehow bind together his television series crowd and the new, emerging television sports fans. He was elegant and reassuring in a milieu that was quietly charged.

The videotaped remarks and presentation for the opening show went off as planned and succeeded on a number of levels. It set up the notion of what cable and satellite did and how they operated. It showed a range of sports—and sometimes the same touchdown over and over (USC scoring on UCLA). With George Grande and Lee Leonard, it showed that sports commentators would offer commentary and opinion. Women's sports would play an important role. This was a send-off that I felt worked, though I had to talk to Bill Rasmussen about his future with ESPN in the next few days before I left, something I didn't look forward to doing.

Later, we stood around and watched *SportsCenter* come on again. I watched the technicians put the tape on to play the softball game. Ironically, one of the featured softball teams was sponsored by Schlitz Beer, which felt strange to us, considering our deal with Budweiser.

Afterward, a group of us went back to the Farmington Inn for drinks and dinner. Everybody was laughing and happy. For a couple of us at least, the mood would change.

In the morning, I met with Bill Rasmussen for breakfast and told him of my plan for Chet Simmons to be chief executive officer. I told Rasmussen that all external contacts for rights acquisitions and press relations would be Simmons' exclusive responsibility. Furthermore, Rasmussen had to arrange to turn in the Cadillacs leased for his son and himself. He took it hard, and while this decision was difficult for me, it was necessary if peace were to come to the executive suite that had become so contentious following the hiring of Simmons.

I flew back to Los Angeles several days later. In the short time I had been in Bristol, I realized how engaged I had become with the staff and, especially, the bright and shining faces of the young people who had been hired to work there. On the other side of plenty was the multitude of questions people scurried up to ask me. Instinctively, people wanted me to do more. When can we have this position filled? When will we get insurance? What's the possibility of another mobile van? As the questions piled up like bad debts, I stood there explaining that we hadn't a budget yet for ongoing operations. Neither had we an employee-relations department or a health plan. When someone, whom everyone construes as Mr. Moneybags, has to tell everyone he doesn't know when—or if—the corporation will have the money, there are plenty of shrugging shoulders, which obviously assign blame. I couldn't talk about the future. Frankly, I just did not know.

At the end of the launch, I was left thinking of the provocative line spoken by Adrian Metcalfe, the British anchor who had appeared on the show. Standing before the River Thames and telling the audience about ESPN's interest in international sports, he said, "It's a frenzied season between summer and winter."

CHAPTER 12

ESPN GOES TO THE MOVIES

The road to Bristol, Connecticut, took me to Acapulco, Mexico; England; and Liberia, Africa. Next, in life's uncertain way, it kept me home. Though I didn't know it at the time, my road was leading me toward another business success: sustaining the recently started ESPN.

On April 23, 1980, a new deal was announced by *Variety* magazine. The headline and article read:

GETTY OIL CO. FEEVEE BOMBSHELL

Getty Oil Company yesterday threw a bombshell into the pay-per-view marketplace, announcing that it was joint venturing a new satellite-delivered national pay-TV service with Columbia Pictures Industries, MCA Inc., Paramount Pictures Corp., and 20th Century Fox Corp.

I hoped that the cable opportunity I saw possible in the Premiere movie deal—or that of ESPN—wouldn't string me along, the way certain skeptical souls maintained that the whole of cable was doing to an increasingly wired country.

The pay cable project brought me in conflict with the cable industry itself. The caption on the cover of the magazine *Watch* (May 1980) read: "Fueling Pay"—an obvious play on words regarding another diverse business opportunity I ended up pursuing, full bore, an effort called Premiere. The illustration showed me mounted on a horse, a knight in armor, gold breastplate and all, holding a miniature gas pump with the hose aimed toward my head. Before me, blocking my path, stood three fellows also in armor, but with red capes, each one labeled with the name of the opposition: HBO, Showtime, and Home Theater Network. Overhead, two satellites floated beneath the arch of the United States Justice Department as leisurely as some child's remote-controlled toys.

Today, I almost get an ominous feeling from looking at what might otherwise seem a playful illustration. Am I intending to turn the hose on myself, immolating myself, becoming a martyr for some cause? It wasn't that bad. Though the effort to create a pay cable service did fail, Premiere was yet another opportunity to hold the reins of a powerful project right alongside of some of the most powerful entertainment people in the world. All of this experience had importance, for if I could strengthen my hand, I could stay ahead of the game and keep ESPN alive. As I gained experience in the television industry, I endured another wild business chase, this time into the area of pay motion pictures.

ESPN had gotten through to the end of a full year, its first, when I got a call from Al Rush. Rush was an old friend of ESPN President Chet Simmons. The two had known each other at NBC before they both left, Rush to take over a job in acquisitions for MCA/Universal Pictures and Simmons to become president of ESPN. "How about lunch on Friday?" Rush asked. "I have something to talk to you about."

We met at the usual place, the Palm in Beverly Hills, and Rush explained the situation involving the movie pay channels: HBO, Showtime, and The Movie Channel. He explained to me the flow of movie product, from theatrical distribution to the other markets: video stores, foreign sales, and one of the biggest, pay cable.

Even though I felt as though I had been there at the creation of cable, and pay movies started about the time ESPN had, cable sports and cable movie channels were worlds apart. By now, though, I was thinking about all aspects of media.

Rush explained that HBO and the other movie pay services were crunching the major studios on the fees they would pay the studios. But the studios did not want to discontinue this distribution, as it still provided them with more money than they would have had otherwise. Still, the issue went beyond money to control, and studios, as with most large corporations, do not like to be controlled. This turnabout came as shocking to the movie channels, possibly because the studio system had evidenced a significant decline in recent years. Indeed, if it wasn't, the meeting with Rush smacked of the last stand for the studios. I had just been through all this with ESPN, and getting involved would allow another major project to take over my life.

Al Rush was a terrific guy. His career at NBC had allowed him to negotiate for television rights for the Olympic Games and had made his now lofty position with MCA/Universal Pictures possible. "Stu," he said, "like it or not, you're in the television business. We think we can put together a group that could start another pay movie service."

"Would Universal be involved then?" I asked.

"Yes, Universal and the other major studios, which account for about 80 percent of the movies made in the United States."

At the beginning of the conversation, I was dividing my thoughts between Rush's words and the pressing matters of the day, including the almost daily requests at ESPN for additional funding. But I could almost feel the adrenaline coursing through my veins as he spoke. Suddenly, I found I'd cleared my head of everything else but what Rush was saying. This was a real idea.

"You think you can get all the studios to work together?"

"It sounds unrealistic, maybe, but they will view it as being in their best interest."

"You used the words 'will view it as . . .'"

"We've already been in touch with a number of studio people. There's virtually no doubt."

"So the plan is . . . ?" I asked.

"ESPN could join together with the major studios. The studios would supply you and your network with feature films. We'll call the network 'Premiere.'"

The prospects excited me so much that I shut up and listened. "So we'd have a direct line at ESPN for pictures?"

"Not only that, you'd get these films 90 days before they were released to any other pay movie service," Rush added.

I must have picked his brain for a half hour more, for I could feel my old desire to know everything about an important project arise. In this instance it mattered especially, because I thought I might at some time, with luck, be in charge. But then, maybe my appetite for a big deal—or for movies—was leading me, not my logic.

I sat there nursing a martini as my mind ticked off the pluses: these were major players, well-capitalized, long-standing corporations, solid, and the creators of real products with real, enduring value. I knew many of the executives that Rush mentioned, some only casually, but all seemed to be solid executives who had vision for their companies and respect from their peers, not to mention track records of success. I felt humbled to find myself in their company, although I recognized it was really ESPN they were after, not me. No matter.

At the time, ESPN management and I were looking around for new avenues to explore that might help sustain the company. We were, after all, ESPN and, as we boasted, with our satellite technology, we could go practically anywhere—not that anywhere necessarily included the boardrooms of the indisputable giants of the motion picture entertainment industry.

"Sounds like a helluva fit," I said. "What's the next step?"

"We'll all need to get together."

I left the meeting thinking of the huge potential success Premiere could be. I still didn't understand the proposition fully, though I had a detailed portrait. I categorized this idea as a "4:00 A.M. thinker." I'd surely be rolling and tossing over it at that time—the later the better. This one was worth plenty of all-nighters. I'd been sleepless lately anyway.

My rational side tried hard to pick at the idea for several days, and it still seemed good, although the line between good and almost-too-good was a razor-thin one, with an emphasis on the razor. Competitors—even they ultimately would be shown in pretty, red capes—could not be expected to react in a gallant way. This was business—their business. HBO, especially, had lived too long as number one in its field, and I knew it would come at us with all the grace of a divorce lawyer.

Finally, though, the concept seemed to be appearing of itself—as if it were magic, ordained. Corporate counsel, internal to the Getty Company, as well as our outside counsel, and a wealth of lawyers in the major studios' legal departments—had originally told us that an antitrust issue could surface, but likely not in an insurmountable way. Whether that was disingenuous lawyer-speak, we couldn't know, but we all put our faith in their judgments and felt as though the world was going to be friendly to us, that Premiere would happen.

If anything could buoy my spirits, it was the group that we put together. Along with Al Rush of Universal, we had what we thought was a formidable team, which included Rich Frank, president of Paramount Pictures Television Distribution; Larry Hilford Sr., vice president of Columbia Pictures Industries; Steve Fox, president of 20th Century Fox Telecommunications; and a guy from Montana named Stuart Evey, the vice president of diversified operations at Getty. The press called us "GOPEC," for Getty Oil Premium Entertainment Channel, a moniker that would evoke, to some, the gas shortages of the seventies and wealthy Saudi oil sheiks.

View: The Magazine of Cable TV Programming, in its September 1980 issue, opined on Burt Harris, whom we had hired as president of our fledgling company. The magazine called Harris "an honorable man" and said that was why we had chosen him. He would, in their words, serve as a kind of "Don Quixote to hold together this impossible dream of an improbable marriage." It must have sounded to some who read the trades like we intended to take over the whole of cable and, after that, quite possibly, the world. *View* had something else to say, which literally made us feel like bastards: "Nobody believed there was a shotgun persuasive enough, an alter encompassing enough, vows individually self-serving enough, to engender and sustain such a union."

Still, our own spokesman, Sid Sheinberg, president of MCA, invoked one of the more emotive arguments of the effort, along with variations on William Shakespeare, when he claimed that the Department of Justice had not gone after Home Box Office in *View.* Unfairness, he implied, had not been served. To that, Sheinberg added, "When somebody comes after an unborn infant while allowing a giant to roam, something stinks in Denmark."

Premiere's rates were similar to HBO's, but the three-month "window," in a sense, blocked the television view, which was a problem for television stations that had coalesced as a group against the idea. They complained bitterly that the delay affected them and their ability to get their programming out. And cable systems, owned by competitors like TelePrompTer, Time, Warner-Amex, and Viacom maintained a unified front. It was big against big, but sometimes the arguments felt lopsided.

It wasn't long before the Justice Department charged in its suit that the Premiere plan violated the Sherman Antitrust Act and, further, that the delay of nine months stood as an "illegal boycott." I attended the federal trial in New York City, where high-priced lawyers on both sides ripped into each other. But the 90-day window kept coming back to haunt us, and we soon came to understand that it may have marked our Achilles heel. The window was something we feared, but not enough to exit from the terms of our proposal.

Premiere vowed to continue, but the government is bigger than even the studios, and we canned the idea. I realized I had to be more interested in the operations of ESPN than the idea of pay cable, but for a shining time, we had a chance at another huge venture. Still, the publicity surrounding the endeavor gained us friends, as well as enemies, but mostly it made Stuart Evey someone with whom to contend. I had sided with some big guys, and they with me, and connections made from the Premiere deal became powerful and influential allies. Under the terms of the Premiere agreement, Getty actually profited from the relationship. Being the "white knight," we were protected from losses and received a management fee for our role.

CHAPTER 13

ADVICE AND CONSENT

Knowledge is a dangerous thing, I realized, when I hired McKinsey and Company, the international management consulting firm, to consult on the issue of ESPN. But I felt I had to do something to quickly reinforce and strengthen the new company. When the original decision was made to go forward with ESPN, I knew I would live to feel the weight of that decision. The need to act or lose the satellite had not allowed adequate time for the "due diligence"—that assiduous research required to underwrite the feasibility of an undertaking. Now, just a year later, I was looking for substantiation and support, but would they come? And if so, how? With the force of a hurricane or a simple windstorm?

McKinsey and Company's effort to develop, plan, and answer some questions was led by Roger Warner, a bright and affable twenty-something graduate of the University of Virginia. In the summer of 1980, when Warner journeyed to Bristol for the first time, the consensus was that, though young, he was an outstanding and talented young man. Warner's background involved developing marketing plans for a number of consumer brands, as well as experience with television and electronic media and advertising. Getty Oil had a long history of using McKinsey as consultants in the past. Traditionally, Getty opted to bring in consultants in cases where we wanted to make one business discrete from some other, or to determine the validity of an idea before a proposal was presented to J. Paul Getty. In one of his many degrading and scathing zingers to his son George, J. Paul Getty made the statement: "In reviewing the results for the company this past year, one could envision a nine-year-old Hottentot doing better." Word from a consultant cut quickly through the intimidation of the old man and immediately heartened the effort. Consultants' reports nearly always put ideas immediately on track—that is, if the results found in any recommendations from the consultant were stout enough.

When we contacted McKinsey and Company for ESPN, we did so out of a need to determine the answers to two important questions: first, I wanted to find out if the satellite cable television industry had any possibility of being viable; second, would an all-sports network have a chance to be viable. But third, fourth, and fifth questions evolved out of the first "diagnostic" answers.

The Bristol, Connecticut, headquarters of ESPN that Roger Warner visited in 1980 consisted of only a few trailers, a studio, and makeshift offices. He didn't know what to expect, other than a large satellite dish or two. What he saw were about 15 to 20 employees and a very small business; he saw the staff doing multiple jobs, effectively performing what he referred to as "the germ of an idea."

McKinsey's gaze into the future of the industry would take time and money, and when completed, Getty Oil and ESPN would have spent $1 million. The unknowns of the cable business were simply nothing to be skirted.

Warner viewed the industry, in general, and ESPN, specifically, as a kind of start-up, with the kinds of problems associated with start-ups. But there was no data to support his understanding. He decided to look at surrogate data to try to find out what ESPN could do. He chose independent television station ratings. Independent television stations were stations not associated with the major networks of the time: CBS, NBC, and ABC. Often recently begun, the independent stations were frequently marginal and sketchy in their operations. They were hopeful, scaled-down versions of regular network stations, which often depended on the flow of syndicated television. Many independents depended on a few staples of syndication, like Gene Roddenberry's *Star Trek* television series, whose 50-something episodes they "turned around" as soon as they had run all of them. Then they'd run them all again.

As the researchers looked at independent stations in major markets with a lot of competition, they found that an average independent station could achieve a two rating, or 2 percent of the total television households between the hours of 6:00 P.M. and 12:00 A.M. Based on that, they figured that an all-sports network, like ESPN, might be narrower. A 1.5–2 rating would likely be the best that we could achieve.

Another issue—how the cable industry itself might grow and evolve—carried its own ethereal notions. Then, too, no cable operation could work efficiently without the receiving locations being wired. Without wire connections, even the satellite-based service would be inoperable. McKinsey sought to determine cable's potential growth by surveying virtually every cable company in America. Specifically, the questionnaire dealt with the markets where the cable system had franchises. How rapidly had each franchise been completed? What was the cost per mile to wire households to cable? What was the cost per customer?

Having hired McKinsey, I was looking forward to an objective review. Later, I began to have some concerns. One of the three partners assigned to us, Sharon Patrick, was a young woman right out of college. She was blonde, attractive, well-educated, and stood well on her feet. She and the others spent a lot of time at ESPN, and every once and a while, those of us at Getty came out of meetings with the feeling that the ESPN management in Bristol was pumping her full of information. She seemed to be picking up their opinion that Getty management was suffocating them with rules, procedures, and constraints, which limited them in "looking, acting, and operating" like a traditional network. She told us we needed more upscale programming and that the more money ESPN had, the better the programming we would receive. I felt I could have said all that. But I didn't have the kind of money that she was suggesting. And we didn't have an audience to justify the additional expenditure at that time. In short, while I may have been incorrect about this, she seemed to be becoming more like a spokesperson for ESPN's management, and less than a detached, dispassionate examiner.

Sometimes, I'd come out of a brief meeting with her and state my old favorite line: "I'm not going to last forever, so I'm not going to listen to *this* sales pitch!"

Clearly, though, it was off-putting for me to think that someone would—by virtue of friendship or proximity—end up taking sides. There were things that I needed to know to help with the rising pressure I had begun to feel from Getty senior management. If anyone would twist the facts, I would, but I didn't really want to put myself in that kind of position.

On December 7, 1980, the anniversary of Pearl Harbor, I flew to New York to meet with our three McKinsey representatives. The meeting was the next day, December 8, the day John Lennon was shot and killed outside his New York apartment. It was a gray, New York day. As we followed the McKinsey people into the conference room at the Getty Oil marketing offices at 660 Madison Avenue, I wanted to be surprised with some new knowledge about cable—not propped up like some tiresome dilettante. Above all, anything I got had to be substantial. I suffered through a minefield of ideas within myself, but these people were experts. As some local business philosopher once said, "I buy advice, you buy opinions." The distinction there may fall to the individual, but I knew the day was about distinctions.

I sensed, from the beginning, uneasiness on the part of Roger Warner and Sharon Patrick. They had better be right, I thought.

"We literally had to do a great amount of soul searching," Roger Warner told me, remembering that meeting. "We knew if we recommended that Getty really buy into this fairly expensive and risky start-up process that it was risky for us and could likely compromise our long and highly profitable relationship with Getty."

During the meeting, as my racing mind struggled to absorb their import, the financial details spewed forth: we would have a five-year plan to reach the break-even point. Ouch! From Warner, I knew that an upside to the scenario existed. Yes, it would take longer, but at the end of the day, a business would exist that was a lot more valuable than anyone had originally thought. The confounding and seductive idea that had circulated among many who launched networks in the late 1970s was that they'd all reek of profits by the second year of operations. Instead, the bottom line reeked—and not with profits. Everybody thought a network could be built on $30 million. Maybe I was one.

Warner weighed his words carefully, knowing full well that ESPN had assets, most notably the transponder on Satcom 1, which had real value. That suddenly put selling the business and its assets in a wonderful light.

We took a break. I remember Warner was nervous and went to the bathroom more often than he should have. I must have been there too, to know he was there. My stomach was in knots. Warner was the same thoughtful, genteel man that I had grown to trust in a very short time, but his nervousness scared me.

He was beginning to tell me what I didn't want to hear. "This can be a great business, but . . ." I needed a magic man who would see that any cracks in the argument were sealed with a quick piece of information as quickly as the smooth swipe of a trowel. We spent some more time looking at statistics, as if any of the minds present could fully incorporate anything requiring more than a yes or no.

Finding a deep breath after hearing that ESPN would need $100 million more—in addition to the five years—was nearly impossible. I don't think anyone in the McKinsey group smoked, but I remember how George Getty said he didn't like negotiating or talking with people who smoked pipes. It wasn't that he opposed smoking so much. Rather, he complained that the pipe smoker would stop to take a puff and would get an extra moment to think before speaking. That seemed, to him, an unfair advantage. Now, I was in a position where I needed about a dozen full pipes going at the ready.

From the McKinsey folks, we learned that ESPN would have to build a significantly larger organization. I knew, as did Warner, that managing the Getty board's expectations would test my credibility. Furthermore, because I had virtually sold the idea for ESPN without the full board of directors, I would have to get them in the loop and soon, for my friends, Director Harold Stuart and Chairman Harold Berg, had presented the idea and told the board: "Ratify this thing." The board had not yet come to grips with the endeavor. When would they? Time was catching up with us. And now the money issue had appeared like an upstart waving his hand at a board meeting, like an illegitimate child that has found you. Who could say no? I couldn't. ESPN was my child. I couldn't stop. I waited for Warner's and the others' final judgment, but it was not a finale. I was left with the sense that the race was a marathon, not a sprint.

Warner later told me, "I probably fell in love with the idea along the way after looking at it for six months. I really wanted to believe it would be successful. But also, I felt a serious concern that I would not let my own personal taste color my judgment." I think I sensed Warner's belief even as he detailed the realities ESPN faced.

I grew more and more intense about ESPN and the need to keep it going—and not all of my reasons were wholesome. Some were outright self-serving. I didn't want ESPN to go away because of what I had said originally to the Getty folks. I could soon be caught dead in the West. How's that for a title of something? *Dead in the West: The Rise and the Fall of a Getty VP*. Though I hadn't lied, I hadn't told the whole truth. There was bad stuff left unsaid, sitting out there for someone to discover.

I worried about my good support network, the Harolds—Berg and Stuart. What would happen to them? The worst bad thing is to bring down one's friends, and they would likely fall with me if everything collapsed. I would often think of Jack "Chappie" Blackburn, fighter Joe Louis' trainer, who said teaching boxing skills to anybody was easy enough, but teaching someone to get up who'd been knocked down was not.

After a meeting where many basic assumptions are challenged, one either folds or begins the wretched task of soul-searching. I did the latter, deciding I needed a major move. Maybe it would involve another media company—a large one, like a network. I didn't know. But I knew I had to face the board. I was convinced that a major corporation would make the board members of Getty Oil Company not just seem satisfied with ESPN and its prospects for the future, but would make them actually smile.

Though I was on the other side of the country from ESPN, personnel problems still nauseated me at times. I had found it necessary, sometimes, to mind Chet Simmons' business as if it were my own—which, in a way, it was. Assuredly, I lacked confidence in him. Over time, even a short time,

I came to think that he was insecure and that he did not have the abilities to run a business of this nature and magnitude. Philosophically, I believe that insecurity—deep-seated insecurity—is one of the great weaknesses because it feeds on itself and creates more and greater problems. It colors how one sees the world. And the world is seen nearly always in relation to oneself. Ego can also be damaging, but one must have some ego to function and to strive. I know I have my share of ego—always did. But I was afraid I would soon have the insecurity to match it.

Chet Simmons was excellent and talented at what he did, which was to get the picture on the air and to work on developing writers and staff who could do a professional sports news program. But when it came to the broader duties, I felt he was lacking. For one thing, he had closed down communication with Getty, including me, and didn't want any of the staff to talk either. I was under huge pressure to replace Simmons with someone else. In fact, in Roger Warner I had a compatriot who tried, at times, to run interference and to keep things from getting too far off the rails.

Further, it wasn't just Simmons, but a lot of the employees had never had the opportunity to manage a totally integrated business. They had experience in their special areas of expertise, whether buying programs or putting them on air, or even selling advertising, but hardly any of them had overall, general management experience in any business. At the time, ESPN was operating without formal budgets and forecasts, which made it tougher for Chet Simmons and for all of us. Being in uncharted waters also exposed everyone to seemingly limitless surprises and needs for capital. Sometimes, undoubtedly, Simmons couldn't get the information or endless funding he needed.

The staff at ESPN was much like that of other start-ups; that is, they were reflections of the original company, if indeed there was one. But the operation closest in resemblance to broadcast television was cable and, besides, most of the people that began working at ESPN in those early days had come from broadcast television—especially NBC. We not only had the broadcast television prototype, but we had one skewed by practices at a vast network operation. This wasn't all bad, however, it led to some false and misleading assumptions. Cable television, for one, could not look just like broadcast television, nor could its financial structure. Originally, the notion, heaped on pages of projections, was that cable would pay its affiliates to carry its signal, and that it would make all its revenues off of one source: advertising sales. At ESPN, we had a lot of people who gave that notion as much credence as a piece of junk mail—people both in programming and sales.

ESPN would be imperiled if we couldn't adapt to a new model, communicate at will, and manage somehow, in tough times, to work together.

CHAPTER 14

Easy as ABC

At about 4:00 A.M. one night in February of 1982, I realized I had to bring in a partner on ESPN or we weren't going to pull it off. A few hours earlier, a peaceful night's sleep had been interrupted by an urgent phone call from Chet Simmons, ESPN's president.

"Stu, Ted Turner's just come in with a $6 million offer. It's take it or leave it—only on the table until tomorrow morning. We've got to come up with another million tonight or we're going to lose the deal."

I knew immediately what he was talking about. Simmons had been in New York for the last two days negotiating with officials of the soon-to-be-announced United States Football League. We thought we had wrapped up a deal for the programming rights at $5 million, but now Turner had come in at the last minute with one million more dollars. If we didn't match Turner's offer, we'd lose the USFL.

The USFL would be the first professional football league to compete against the National Football League since 1972, when the American Football League merged with the NFL. Chet and I were in agreement, for once, that securing the rights to their games would be a major coup for ESPN. We were trying to sign them up to a two-year deal for programming rights to televise a package of their games on Sundays. Based on preliminary discussions with the USFL's television committee, Simmons had determined that the package would cost us between $4.5 and $5 million.

Five million dollars was very big money for ESPN in those days. In fact, it was the largest sum we'd ever offered for a single programming package. I knew that we'd never make money on the deal, but I also knew it was a slam-dunk for us. The publicity alone would be worth the price. The new league wasn't announcing its formation until May, but the sports pages were already talking about it. The league was well funded, and its 12 franchises would be located in major markets across the country, including New York, Los Angeles, Chicago, Detroit, Boston, Denver, Washington, and Philadelphia.

It was still minor league compared to the NFL, but that had its advantages. The major networks wouldn't be interested. The USFL owners were anxious to nail down a television contract and make it part of their announcement. That was fine with us because we were anxious to be named as the league's network when play began in the spring of 1983.

The USFL went on to fulfill our greatest expectations. It generated huge fan interest before the first season by signing the likes of Heisman Trophy winner Herschel Walker, who would have been the first pick in the NFL draft that year. The initial USFL season was our highest-rated series ever, and, for the next five years, franchise owners like Donald Trump kept the fans coming to the stadiums—and tuning into ESPN—by raiding the NFL for star players. In fact, Trump became a real headache to ESPN's programming office during the USFL's brief life. Always nagging Bill Grimes, who succeeded Chet Simmons as president later in 1982, Trump tried to put his team, the New Jersey Generals, on the air. He finally called me to complain. I told him that we had to show games in accordance with the contract we had with the league. "I'm sorry, Don. We can't make any exceptions."

Trump, who had angered his fellow owners by not conforming to the league's rules that limited signings of star players for the sake of competitive balance, exploded at me: "Goddamn it, it's my money that's keeping this league alive. I should get more games!"

But that was a year down the road. Now Chet Simmons was telling me that the asking price was another million dollars. And that was a big problem. "Can we do it, Stu?" Simmons implored. "It's still a great deal for us."

I agreed that it was still worth it, even with the extra million—and there was no way I was going to let Ted Turner get the rights ahead of us. TBS was still the biggest cable network in terms of viewership, but we were catching up fast. Getting the USFL would get us up even faster. If Turner beat us out for the rights, it could very well add another year or more to TBS's primacy in the cable universe.

At a time when the advertising industry still looked down at cable as the ugly stepchild of broadcast television, being number one translated into advertising money. It was no secret that advertisers who were considering cable tended to go with TBS as their default cable option for the simple reason that it had the largest viewership. I wanted to win that place in advertisers' hearts for ESPN, and I wasn't about to let $1 million keep it from my grasp. So I was willing enough to give Simmons the go-ahead, but there was one big problem: I didn't have the authority to raise the offer by another million dollars.

At a typical television network, a network president could have swung approval for the extra money in a matter of hours or made the decision himself. But ESPN was Getty Oil property. The oilmen who controlled the company may have agreed to back the ESPN venture and put me in charge, but that didn't mean they trusted me to spend their money as I saw fit. My bosses thought of me as somewhat of a loose cannon, and senior management had determined they should keep a tight leash on my pet project. They'd even recently assigned a new corporate attorney, Dave Henri, from another Getty subsidiary to head my legal team, a move my lawyer was to tell me months later that was made "to keep Stu from going off the deep end with ESPN." The upshot was that the ESPN budget, and any major changes in the budget, required the approval of Getty's chief financial officer and the board of directors.

I'd spent a lot of time planning my original request for the funding to bid on the USFL television rights. My presentation to the Getty board of directors was peppered with advertising sales statistics and tales of the commercial success generated by the American Football League when it was an upstart league vying with the NFL. With the backing of Getty president Harold Berg and chief financial officer Sid Petersen, the board gave us approval to bid up to $5 million for the rights.

Bidding above the board-approved budget for the USFL rights meant going back to the board and amending the budget. Eventually, it would get done, but the board of directors only met quarterly, and they weren't about to convene a special session just to hear me ask for more money. It would take time to convince my oilmen that the USFL was well worth an extra million dollars, and time was clearly something we didn't have.

I told Simmons I'd get right back to him, but the truth was I didn't know what to do. Gears spinning, I decided to call Jerry Salomon. Salomon was the president of the D'Arcy McManus Agency, the advertising agency representing ESPN's largest advertiser, Anheuser-Busch. Salomon had been an early believer in ESPN and was instrumental in getting Budweiser to sign our first big sponsorship deal before we launched in 1979. After apologizing for the late hour, I told him my problem: "Jerry, I hate to ask you this, but I'm stuck. Do you think you can get Anheuser-Busch to put up the extra money so we can get this thing?"

He thought about it a minute. "Let me make a call. I'll have an answer for you in the next hour." He called me back in 40 minutes. "Stu, Anheuser-Busch will give you half a million. But your announcers had better mention Budweiser every five minutes during those football games."

The Anheuser-Busch money was a big help, but only got me halfway there. I could make more calls and try to dig up more cash from outside sources. But given the time frame, not to mention the time of night, it probably would be fruitless. That left me with two options: give up on the deal or give Simmons the go-ahead and take my chances with Getty. It was crunch time. I called Simmons. "OK. Do it. Raise our offer to $6 million."

"Great. I'll tell them."

"You can also tell them if they ask for another penny," I growled, "I can't make it happen." An hour later, he called back to tell me we had the rights.

I didn't bother trying to get back to sleep. I got in to work early and camped out in front of Harold Berg's office. When he came in, I grabbed him. "Harold, I've got to talk to you. It's about the USFL deal." I told him what had happened, that we'd had to make the commitment last night or lose the rights. I made sure to tell him how I'd gotten Budweiser to put up half. In the end, he told me not to worry, that he'd make sure it went smoothly with the board.

But I knew after that night that we couldn't go on operating like this. The further along we got with ESPN, the more often things like this would be happening, and even bigger money would be involved. I was risking my career every time a quick financial decision was required. Eventually, we were going to either lose a programming deal that we really wanted, or I was going to be raked over the coals by my superiors at Getty for authorizing expenditures I wasn't authorized to make.

The money itself wasn't the problem. The amounts being invested in ESPN were small potatoes for a company like Getty, which in 1981 had an operating cash flow of $2.7 billion. Still, profits had been down the previous year and looked worse in the current year. Operating a peripheral, unproven business with steady losses at a time when fortunes were at low ebb did not exactly make me the most popular man at the company. In fact, it was about that time that a joke started circulating around Getty headquarters that was directed at my regular advocacy for more money: ESPN really stood for the Evey Sports Programming Network. Believe me, it was not meant to be complimentary. Outside of my diversified operations group, Getty people didn't particularly believe in ESPN. It had started out as a novelty, but the novelty was wearing thin with every passing month of losses.

It was clear to me, as it would have been to any media executive, that we had to keep growing the business. Our subscriber base continued to expand, and we knew we were gaining new viewers at a fast pace. *Cable TV News* had recently named ESPN the cable network with the greatest "lift," meaning cable subscribers requested our network be made available more than any other cable station. Unfortunately, we couldn't back up the indications of our increasing viewership with the hard numbers the advertising industry was waiting for. That kind of statistical evidence would have to wait until ACNielsen deemed our audience large enough to rate.

It was a catch-22. Building our subscriber base up to numbers at which ACNielsen would start rating us meant spending more money on better programming in order to attract those viewers. But Getty was reluctant to keep spending more—and losing more—money until we could show solid proof that our bottom line was improving. Standing still meant falling behind, and we didn't have much room to slide back. I was walking a tight rope, trying to balance the needs of my people back in Bristol against the demands of Getty people in Los Angeles. It was an uncomfortable way to operate, to say the least. I was beginning to worry about how much further I could pull Getty into the sports network before my career was jeopardized.

Getty had already spent nearly $50 million on top of its original $10 million investment. ESPN had recently hit a "burn rate"—the amount of cash flowing out above and beyond the cash from revenues flowing in—of $8 million per month. That was an alarming number. If we kept burning through Getty money at that rate, our losses on ESPN would nearly double in six months and reach $150 million by the end of 1982. Those kinds of numbers would not escape the attention of Berg's office or the board of directors. Those were the kind of numbers, in fact, that could finish ESPN and lose me my job. I feared being out in the world, hat in hand, in a marginal economy, having helped bring down a giant corporation—not a pretty prospect for a guy who'd given his all for the corporate team Getty.

Back in 1979, when I'd gone to the board with my first request for more money to keep ESPN afloat, I'd said, "Gentleman, I promise you I will never take us in further on ESPN than I can safely get us out." I had a long record of making money for Getty with unlikely ventures, and they believed me. That promise held true until Getty's investment reached $50 million. In the short time since Bill Rasmussen had leased ESPN's original satellite transponder for $1 million per year in 1978, the going rate had soared to $30 million. We owned the rights to two transponders now. I could recoup our investment thus far by selling our transponder rights. But ESPN required more investment from Getty every month, and I had no idea whether I could get Getty out of ESPN in a year's time without taking heavy losses.

Getty's relationship with ESPN had reached the breaking point. I knew I couldn't give the people in Bristol the money they needed to make ESPN a better network. The next step was clear: we needed to partner with people who knew their way around a television network, understood how a network operated, and had a feel for—and a tolerance of—the kind of expenditures needed to make it successful. The logical choice was an affiliation with one of the major networks. It made sense. But that didn't mean it was going to be easy. The big three broadcast networks had a love-hate relationship with cable television that was more love than hate at that time. But we did have our own talented people who could call the shots under great pressure and spur ESPN to at least maintain the kind of profile it needed to attract such a partner. At the helm was the focused and often prickly Chet Simmons.

While ESPN sportscaster Chris Berman would light up like a Christmas tree when he mentioned the New York Giants or Philadelphia Eagles, his favorites, I knew not to expect a lot of enthusiasm from Chet Simmons about sports—or business, for that matter, including what I considered some key deals. I figured he wasn't going to bubble over about the Premiere movie venture with the studios, and he didn't. I thought he'd appear less irritated at the posting of the $1 million bond for the 1984 Olympics. Simmons viewed that Olympian effort as little more than a ridiculous publicity stunt—one that degraded the network to boot.

Obviously, Simmons and I had our differences. But what grew increasingly irritating to me and to management, including Scotty Connal, was the negative cast in which Simmons viewed so many new ideas. And ESPN was a very big new idea.

Whenever I was suggesting some new direction, tactic, or ploy, I felt like an outsider trying to break in, even though I was officially the boss. The term that, oddly enough, comes to mind in relation to Simmons is "cowcatcher." A cowcatcher was an announcement that took place in the beginning of early broadcasts to try to sell something other than the main sponsor's product. It seemed I was always trying to sell something else.

Simmons had his way of doing things, and new ideas—often what I thought of as creative ideas—would typically meet with his disdain.

Sometimes I was even right—incontrovertibly right, at least, if the idea's ultimate acceptance is any measure. In a memo to Chet Simmons dated September 16, 1981, I wrote:

> Congratulations on a good weekend. I'll be interested in the overnight ratings for the football game. While watching the Oregon game on Saturday, Dan Burke and I were discussing the possibility of imposing the game score on the screen so that the audience would always be current on the status of the game. Since our audience is low at this time, it would seem that experiments like this, and other innovations, might be interesting. Let me know what you think.

I signed the note and, several days later, received Simmons' answer on the bottom of my note. My secretary wrote:

> Chet called and said that showing the scores will not work. Detracts from game for viewer, and announcers are instructed to give scores at least once every two minutes.

Today, superimposing scores on the television screen has become the norm for many television sports presentations. At the time, I was surprised at his response. I thought—and still think—that Simmons didn't understand a lot about sports in his deepest self. And the love of sports truly lies deep in the souls of real fans. I wondered if he had ever felt the suspense and anticipation of returning to the television where the drama of the game was unfolding, only to have to wiggle and wait for the do-or-die information we call scores. If he had, he might have been a little more accepting of the idea, which is a small example, maybe. I assume the idea of keeping the scores before the audience resulted from others, but I am pleased to have a letter documenting that I was perhaps among the first to try to implement what was, if I do say so, an excellent idea.

On the face of it, we were different—Simmons and I—too different. I was a corporate guy; Simmons was the sports executive. I was flamboyant, preferring to wear sporty colors and to play golf, neither of which he really cared for much. My overall feeling is that what made the two of us so different were our opposite perspectives on life and living.

I don't want to suggest that Simmons didn't offer up ideas. He did. He wanted to expand ESPN into regional areas in the country, for one. Movers and shakers in business all have their own styles, and sometimes the chosen—or divinely conferred—style is not altogether reasoned, decent, or fair.

I insistently sought to keep track of what had occurred on the ESPN broadcasts I received by satellite on my Los Angeles office television. Still, it goes without saying that I constantly needed to be appraised about what was going on in Bristol. At some point, I came to depend too much on the television set for my information. I had become, of necessity, a business couch potato. Though I made calls to Bristol on a daily basis and many of the executives were marvelous and forthcoming, I still needed more direct communications, a more open dialogue with Chet Simmons, and I was left with what I could glean from my television. Call someone else? "Not so fast, my friend," as ESPN's sportscaster Lee Corso would say. Unfortunately, because of his position, Simmons could answer certain things that no one else could.

I believe communication is not just the name of the game—communication is the game! And Simmons didn't want to play. I've often thought how much of communication is simply the desire to communicate. People who work to communicate risk standing accused of redundancy or arrogance, which has occasionally been said of me. Such people need solid, even buttressed, egos, and I was therein blessed. All right, so I repeat myself. But with careful communication, the likelihood of a total misfire is reduced.

Anyway, Simmons, with his baleful and secretive moods, somehow made me feel as though I were some sort of predator—or worse, scavenger—always stalking what I needed: information, figures. By 1981, I knew I needed to do something about Chet Simmons, as outstanding as he was in many ways. But what could I do? I didn't want to let him go outright. I wanted him to land in some other job. But I couldn't abide the situation with him at ESPN any longer. He would have to go, and I'd have to figure out how.

Suddenly, one day, out of the blue, I received a call from my good friend Bill Daniels. He told me he attended the USFL's owners meeting, and they discussed potential candidates for the league commissioner's position. He said Chet Simmons was of interest, and Daniels told them he would call me to explore Simmons' availability. As a courtesy, he said, "I'd like your permission to talk to Chet about the USFL job."

I was flabbergasted and expressed concern about losing Simmons, but I told Daniels that I would not stand in the way of Simmons furthering his career. When I hung up, I bowed my head. My private prayers had been answered.

On June 14, 1982, the United States Football League named Simmons as commissioner.

I knew we'd miss Simmons' reputation and relationships, which were invaluable, but I wished him well. He had made great contributions to ESPN, and I wanted him to succeed. I felt the slow linger of sadness in my mind about our relationship and dealings. Still, it was for the best. ESPN had to go on, and I believed that Simmons would have had a deleterious effect on ESPN's rise to far greater levels. But he went on to perhaps more appropriate climates and soon played a key role in the early success of the USFL. And he left after imparting to ESPN an admirable reputation in the burgeoning industry of cable television.

In the late sixties, the broadcast networks, recognizing that cable television presented a threat to their dominance of the airwaves, successfully lobbied the Federal Communications Commission to prevent cable from coming to the nation's largest one hundred cities. They based their arguments on the grounds that cable threatened the public's right to free television. In 1972, the FCC repealed its earlier rulings, and cable slowly began to fulfill the broadcasters' fears of costing them their chokehold on the nation's viewing audience.

When I had set my people to researching the cable business back in 1978, we came away with the impression that cable programming was poised to break out. Nationally, Home Box Office and Ted Turner's WTBS Superstation had established programming beachheads on cable television. They were developing a loyal following of viewers hungry for an alternative to the programming force-fed to them by the networks.

Still, the prevailing attitude amongst the commercial networks was that the public wouldn't be willing to pay for programming they were getting for free. That attitude especially held true for sports, despite the success of regional sports cable networks like the New York Sports Channel, and the Madison Square Garden Network, which featured New York's local hockey and basketball teams. But by the time ESPN launched in 1979, executives at ABC, NBC, and CBS were beginning to fully appreciate the competitive challenge cable posed to network television. One of those executives was ABC chairman Leonard Goldenson, whom I knew socially through our mutual involvement in the Los Angeles chapter of the United Cerebral Palsy Foundation.

At a UCP meeting just a few months after ESPN's first cablecast, Goldenson pulled me aside. "How are you managing with Simmons and his crew?"

"It's a different world," I told him. "But I'm learning."

"You've got the right idea with ESPN. But when you Getty folks get tired of playing at being television people, you let me know. Maybe I'll take it off your hands for you."

I laughed. "Maybe we'll be able to do the same for you some time."

But Goldenson had seen the light, and ABC was the leader among the majors in getting involved in cable programming. He established a division, ABC Video Enterprises, devoted to providing programming for cable and other alternative distribution media, such as video and pay-per-view. By 1981, ABC had launched its first cable network, ARTS. Soon after, NBC's parent company, RCA, started the Entertainment Channel. The two would later merge to become the Arts and Entertainment Network.

The major broadcast networks were making their first, tentative investments in cable TV programming. Their executives knew that cable was not going to fade away. Still, ABC, CBS, and NBC remained wary and more than a little contemptuous of cable programming. They did not want to anger their local affiliate stations by creating competition for them. So if I were to engineer an advantageous partnership deal with one of the networks, I would have to avoid the perception that I was coming to them with my hat in my hands. I probably could have made a phone call to Goldenson and persuaded ABC to take a piece of ESPN. But then the deal would be made on his terms. I wanted some financial and operational support; I didn't want to turn ESPN over to ABC, or make Getty a junior partner in a company that I'd worked so hard to build. I wanted them coming to me.

Given ESPN's miserable financial situation, it was going to be difficult to swing a partnership deal with a major network on my terms. But in the television business, egos are often as important as bottom lines. In television, perception often has as much to do with success as reality. None of the networks wanted to appear as though they were slipping behind the others. Bragging rights led to publicity, which produced higher ratings.

I intended to play those egos off one another in order to drum up interest in partnering with ESPN. It was a chancy idea, one that could easily backfire. But I was used to that. The biggest of those egos belonged to Roone Arledge, who had built a huge reputation as a brilliant innovator running ABC's sports and news programming divisions. He was responsible for creating *Wide World of Sports* and *Monday Night Football* and for bringing the Olympic games to ABC. From what I could see, however, Arledge's interest in ESPN was minimal—perhaps on the order of a fly on an elephant's back. But I figured that if someone like Roone Arledge heard that another broadcast network was courting Getty to get in on ESPN, he'd get interested himself.

I decided to leak a rumor that Getty might be interested in selling ESPN.

The best person I knew to get a good rumor started in the television industry was Ed Hookstratten. He was the powerful Hollywood and TV agent who'd advised me to steal Chet Simmons away from NBC and make him ESPN's first president. Hookstratten was on retainer with Getty as a consultant. I decided that it was time for him to start earning his pay. I called him and told him we needed to talk.

We met at the Los Angeles Club on the top floor of the Getty building during the heyday of two—and three—martini lunches. The bar area had four booths, one of which was my personal domain. I often met people there for business. I liked the clubby atmosphere, and I liked doing deals with a drink in my hand.

Hookstratten sat himself down across from me. "What's up, Stu?"

"Do you think one of the networks would be interested in buying ESPN?"

He just stared at me for a moment. "Jesus, Stu. Are you serious? What are you talking about exactly?"

That's where I had to tread carefully. I needed Hookstratten's help to drop the lure, but I knew he wouldn't go so far as to knowingly set up people like Roone Arledge or his counterparts at NBC and CBS, Don Ohlmeyer and Neal Pilson. These were the men at the top of the food chain from which Hookstratten feasted. If word were to get out that he had participated in a scheme to manipulate them, his name would be shit in television. Hookstratten was a friend, and I didn't like having to manipulate him, but I decided I didn't have a choice.

"I don't know exactly. It's nothing definite yet," I told him. "You know we've been taking a lot of losses lately, and I think the board is starting to get antsy. They might want to start thinking about getting out of the television business. I just want to be out in front if that happens." Hookstratten absorbed this in silence. "What do you think? Would the networks be interested—if we were to be interested in selling, that is, which is far from definite?"

"I don't know, Stu. It's certainly a possibility."

"I'd like to seed a rumor that we might be thinking of selling, to gauge the amount of interest out there without actually having to say anything definitively. Can you make some calls, get the word out to the people who would be interested?"

Hookstratten agreed, but he didn't want to involve NBC. Most of his top clients, including Tom Brokaw, Bryant Gumbel, and Don Ohlmeyer, were there, and he didn't want to jeopardize his relationship with the network. So it would come down to ABC and CBS. That was fine with me. ABC was the most aggressive and innovative network, and CBS, with the Tisch money behind it, had very deep pockets.

After the debacle over securing the rights to televise the new United States Football League—when I had to beg, borrow, and almost steal—I was feeling like I'd had already had more bumps than a greyhound on the first turn. Now, I had to do something about it. I knew Getty wouldn't carry a television broadcasting network for too long. It wasn't the oil giant's style. The very nature of television recognizes that rights fees for programming is paramount and often requires split-second decisions which, if not executed, can preclude key opportunities for some time in the future and mean severe repercussions for the stability of the network. Major financial decisions, particularly those that require short time frames, were not Getty's mode of operation. Decisions on digging wells or investing in new tankers took weeks, not days or hours. Though it worked for oil and gas investments, that approach didn't work for the constantly and radically shifting world of media business. I used to feel at Getty like we were back in biology class, and if we couldn't study it under the microscope, we couldn't find it. The world was an amoeba or a euglena.

I didn't want to let ESPN go under for personal reasons, but I recognized that the McKinsey study had made the point that success was further out in the future than originally projected. I needed a cushion, and I knew Getty's patience would wear thin with continuing losses. The prospect of classifying ESPN as a dry hole could be sooner rather than later.

Again, I called Ed Hookstratten. If there are six degrees of separation between the average person and Kevin Bacon—or anybody in the world, for that matter, as the popular idea has it—there were many fewer separations between much of the celebrity world if you happened to know Hookstratten and could enlist his help.

"Could you call Roone Arledge and see if ABC would have any interest in exploring possibilities for forming a relationship with ESPN?"

"Are you serious?" Ed said.

"Kind of," I said, revealing a rare—and certain—trace of uncertainty.

Hookstratten questioned me for a while. I found myself coming back with words like, "I'm not sure." I wasn't used to talking like this. In fact, I felt in those moments like the world's poorest salesman, not someone who had always taken pride in mastering those business twins—the gift of gab and the play of negotiation.

"If you want to explore it, go ahead," I said. To this day, I don't know how seriously Hookstratten took me, but I knew he would enjoy this opportunity to speak with the legendary Roone Arledge on matters other than the entertainment and sports talent he represented.

After Hookstratten called Arledge, it wasn't long before Arledge called me. He sounded tired or bored, maybe. "I understand you're about to give up on the lousy business we're in," he said.

"Where'd you hear that?"

"I got word that you guys were tired of television."

"Not at all," I said. "We just secured the rights to the USFL, our first live professional programming, and things are looking quite a lot better."

Arledge had a way of sounding serious, even when he was only partly so—more like coy. "We're not really interested in getting cable," he said. "Our network affiliates, for one thing, wouldn't be too happy if we were to share our expertise and programming with cable television interests. Also, we don't really think delayed or taped sports events on cable television is going to be major factor . . . but since I had heard that you might be discouraged from your foray into the business, I thought I would give you a call."

I told Arledge I appreciated the call and that should there be an interest in the future, I would let him know.

I knew that Hookstratten represented Phyllis George, the gorgeous Miss America of 1971. She had become a top talent at CBS, and I figured that he might make inroads at CBS through her, if not through his regular connections. Additionally, I asked him, "Why not call Gene Jankowski at CBS and see if they have an interest?" I suggested to Hookstratten that he drop the information on Jankowski that I had recently received a call from Roone Arledge about a possible interest in ESPN. Jankowski was group vice president of CBS television. So Hookstratten called Jankowski, and Jankowski rushed to call me.

"I understand you might have an interest in getting out of the business," he said, for openers.

"I don't know where that's coming from," I said. About this time, I let slip that Roone Arledge had called me about ESPN, saying he had heard the same thing. I did that on purpose because I figured—with what I knew of the men—that I was onto something. I knew the two men's personalities and that neither would want the other getting anything over him: type A plus type A equals B, as in a *bidding war*. And I was already suited up for battle.

"Listen," Jankowski said, "don't make any moves before you talk to us."

I knew then that I had the game afoot. I had seen plenty of business people suffer in the past by not keeping the communication open, especially when they had to about-face on a deal they had spoken for and promoted so loudly. I wasn't about to have that happen, but I also didn't know what would happen in the corporate halls if I did. I needed to find out.

One morning, I arranged for a meeting with the chairman of the board of Getty Oil Company and Chief Financial Officer Sid Petersen, and I tried to feel them out about what I was about to do. I thought that if I could assuage any ill feelings that might erupt in the meeting, I would not be blind sided or second-guessed later.

"I've got this deal moving," I opened, nervously. "If I carry on, I might not be able to stop it."

"Someone's interested in ESPN?"

"Yes, there is interest," I said. I must have gulped hard at this juncture. "Do you have any objections if I carry on these discussions . . . recognizing they could lead to an equity participation?"

I further explained that it was my idea to get someone to buy a minority interest in ESPN. For that, we'd get the cash that would help finance the operation for some time into the future. More importantly, we also might end up with a big name—a powerhouse in sports television, which could only enhance our credibility.

"By all means, go ahead," was the response I welcomed from Berg and Petersen.

I called Arledge back and hit him with the absurdity of the rumor idea again. "I know this damn rumor's going around, but if you want to come out and talk to us, I'd be glad to meet with you."

"What do you think you want to do?" Arledge asked.

"I'll probably sell an option to buy into ESPN. We don't want to sell the company—if we're interested at all."

"How much are we talking about?" he questioned.

I laid it out for him: "We have transponders, buildings, and mobile units, and are showing steady growth with cable operators. These are substantial assets that can either be used by others, or liquidated, should that benefit the participating partners."

The well-poised silence at the end of the phone line did not escape my attention. God, he was good!

"It's not that they are worthless," I burst in. Arledge was getting impatient, I could tell.

"Well, how much?" he asked.

"Maybe $10 million to make any transaction worthwhile, but how much that would buy would have to be determined . . . assuming we would have an interest."

"I'll let our guys know," he said.

Upon hanging up, I sat there, exhausted.

Sometime during the next few days, I heard from Herb Granath of ABC Video Enterprises, who had heard from Arledge and was, at least on the surface, interested.

Granath and Fred Pierce, ABC's executive vice president, made arrangements to fly out to see me about the deal. In the meantime, I needed to call Jankowski at CBS while I tried to keep the ball in the air, flying as it was, just within reach among us all. I told him, "The ABC brass are coming out to talk to me. Do you have any interest in seeing this thing further along?"

Jankowski soon had his number one sports guy, Neal Pilson, at his side. "What are you talking about for money?" Jankowski asked.

I told him the numbers had not been thoroughly discussed, and that we were merely feeling out the currents at the time. I had a time-tested caveat, though, which I shuffled into the mix. "Being a potential equity sale, I will have to present an idea of this nature to our executive management." It was my own personal back door, a kind of escape clause.

In the next week or so, Pierce and Granath came out and met with me, attorney Dave Henri, executive assistant Dan Burke, and finance officer Lou Rambau. We spent the better part of the morning hashing over the deal and weighing the positives for both parties. They asked how much it would cost. Then I jumped in, determinedly reminding them that CBS was in the negotiation too. "We're talking about a minority interest at $2 million a point. We'd like to sell 10 percent immediately, with an option to purchase up to 49 percent in five years."

"I thought it was $10 million," Pierce said.

"We've kind of decided that we would sell 10 percent for $2 million a point."

"Oh," Pierce said. We continued talking it over for a while, and then Pierce suddenly jumped up: "Can we use a phone?"

I said, "Sure."

I escorted the men to a private phone and they called—I learned later—Leonard Goldenson, chairman of ABC. They told him the asking price, apparently, and must have explained that CBS was strongly interested. Goldenson told them to offer $20 million.

In the time it would take to make a slap shot at the net, I called Jankowski and told him of the offer. He was pleasant, but I could tell he was disappointed. "We couldn't have done that amount anyway," he said, resigned.

I felt sorry for him in a way. But it was a negotiation. "I said I'd call you, and I did," I reminded him. We hung up.

I had another deal I had discussed with several others, and I needed to explore it with ABC. The ideal time for further discussion was soon, before the climate for negotiation had passed. When I got together with the ABC people again and told them that Getty had accepted the option deal contingent upon a side deal being made on securing programming from ABC, they looked puzzled and somewhat put out, as if supplying ESPN with money and their name was enough. Was I asking too much? I would soon see.

ESPN was the great devourer of sports programming. The "insatiable appetite," as I would say—needed more and more hours to fill the 8,760 hours per year needed for a 24/7 network. We had been on the air 24 hours a day for nearly three years. I was convinced that ABC, with its flagship program, *Wide World of Sports*, would offer great programming potential. After all, *Wide World* would usually broadcast the highlights of a sporting event—skating, skiing, or whatever. We could televise as much as we wanted of an event they didn't use. Furthermore, *Wide World's* producers could shoot additional footage—more than they might need themselves—for distribution to ESPN.

Over a period of time, negotiations for the programming were contentious—if not ugly. But because we had not yet finalized the option deal, and because ABC was so anxious to get in ahead of CBS, they gave in. We finally settled on several classifications of programming, which we referred to as *A*, *B*, and *C*. ABC agreed that ESPN would get so many hours of *A* programming, so many hours of *B* programming, and so many hours of *C* programming at predetermined rates. Some of the programming came free; some was extremely reasonable—especially considering what it would have cost to produce that kind of programming ourselves. Of course, it wouldn't have been available to ESPN without the fortuitous affiliation with ABC.

Good programming immediately grew out of our new liaison. We began showing Thursday and Friday golf by getting the British Open rights for those days from ABC because they only televised the Saturday and Sunday action. We would air 12 hours of programming. That began the Thursday and Friday golf on television, which is so much a part of today's golf programming. ABC benefited too because it was able to pair *Monday Night Football* with two games on ESPN later in the week, which helped it maintain profitability.

In Goldenson's book, *Beating the Odds*, Fred Pierce penned what sounds to me like a left-handed compliment: "Stu Evey was a tough, unique individual." I don't know if I was tough or not, but I knew we had something of value, and I wasn't willing to give it away.

The earlier question about the worth of the company being $2 million per point was a fair enough question. But I wasn't about to tell anybody I'd created the number out of thin air. I had little choice, really. Going by numbers alone would be an exercise in futility. How do you fairly value a company like ESPN in 1982? We had lost $60 million, managed only slow revenue growth, and were burning through another $8 to $10 million each month. On the other hand, the most crucial variable for measuring a television network's success—viewership—was growing at anything but an incremental pace: in less than three years, we had quadrupled the number of homes that could tune in to ESPN. The buzz in the industry had us approaching the breakthrough point in audience numbers that would net us the all-important ACNielsen ratings measurement.

There had been no comparable sales of a cable network either, so I was effectively setting the market for a cable television network. I certainly didn't intend to come cheap. At $2 million per point, I figured that selling 49 percent of ESPN would almost cover Getty's investment thus far and still leave us with majority ownership. But Jankowski and company were only interested in making a financial commitment to ESPN if Getty ceded management control to CBS. That was a deal breaker for me, but I didn't tell them; I needed to keep the pot brewing. Before the CBS team left Los Angeles, I told them I would consider their terms and get back to them.

The people at ABC and Getty shook on the deal before they left Los Angeles. The next week, it hit the headlines. The biggest network in television was coming onboard the ESPN train. You don't think my board of directors suddenly loved me? For a 10 percent share, I'd doubled our original $10 million investment, and now we had a property that was suddenly valued at $200 million, 75 percent of which was ours.

Overnight, the attitude at Getty changed dramatically. ESPN was no longer the Evey Sports Programming Network. Now it was, "Getty's in the

TV business—aren't we clever?" "Another miracle by Evey," someone whispered to me at Getty, as if selling my prize wasn't tearing me emotionally. Yet, everyone from the board of directors on down was excited about ABC's involvement. This was as clear a validation as I could have gotten. And for me personally, the best thing was that I could present it to Getty on a silver platter. I had done this deal, the whole thing, on my own. It was one of the most memorable achievements of my long career. It truly saved ESPN and made the risk I had taken with Getty's money look brilliant.

Over at ABC, however, the feeling weren't quite as mutual. Although we announced the deal jointly in March, the agreement wasn't signed for another six months. ABC's lawyers kept trying to make small changes in the agreement. Most of their demands were trivial: raising the price for the programming they would sell us, the years on the option. Every time they came up with a new demand, I'd tell Dave Henri, who was negotiating the details, to agree to them so we could sign a contract and get the money.

After yet another week had passed without an agreement, I called Henri into my office. "What the hell's going on with this agreement, Dave? I want to get this thing rolling. Is this a case of a bunch of goddamn lawyers doing bullshit haggling, or is this deal going to fall apart?" Henri had just returned from what had turned into a monthly negotiating trip to New York.

"They're pissed off, Stu."

"Why?"

"I think ABC has gone back and taken a hard look at the deal, and they feel like you pulled one over on them. A lot of ABC people, especially Arledge, feel like they paid too much and gave away too much. They're coming back at us with all these little demands because they're pissed off about being out-negotiated."

"Well for Christ's sake," I told him. "Massage their wounds and get that damn contract signed. I need it by the quarterly meeting." The Getty board of directors met every three months, and I didn't feel like explaining to them why we still didn't have the ABC money in hand nearly six months after announcing the deal.

Finally, we inked the contract. It was titled the *Advance and Option Agreement Between ABC Video Enterprises, Inc., American Broadcasting Companies, Inc., ESPN and Getty Oil Company.* The contract was signed by Herb Granath, Fred Pierce, and Bill Grimes of ABC, and by S. W. Evey of Getty Oil Company.

The signing date was August 9, 1982.

ABC threw a signing party at the Tavern on the Green in New York. There were 30 or so people present that evening, most of whom were from ABC. There were five of us from Getty and ESPN: David Henri, Dan Burke, Ron Doutt (my division's financial manager), Ed Hookstratten, and myself. The ABC contingent included its chairman, Leonard Goldenson; ABC's executive president, Fred Pierce; president of ABC Video, Herb Granath; the executive producer of ABC Sports, Roone Arledge; and Howard Cosell, president of the world and everything else.

The mood at our table was downright giddy that night. I was so excited that I felt like dancing with my shoes off. And why not? We finally had a partner contributing money, and there was all that juicy programming that ABC didn't use to which we had access. Most of the ABC folks seemed pleased too, but Arledge and his people clearly were not. He was visibly unhappy to be there.

Over dessert, we toasted our new union. When it was my turn, I congratulated everyone involved for a deal well done. Then I raised my glass to Arledge. "And Roone," I said, "I especially want to take this opportunity to welcome you to big-time sports broadcasting."

Everyone burst into laughter, everyone except Arledge, who didn't even crack a smile. He sat at the table stone-faced, his big, fat cigar burning to ash in his fingers.

Later that evening, several of us took a horse-drawn buggy ride around Central Park, past the elegant Plaza and St. Moritz Hotels, where I wanted desperately to have a few drinks and relax. In the buggy, I was seated with Ed Hookstratten and Roone Arledge. Hookstratten and I spoke enthusiastically about our new partnership, but Arledge didn't say a word the entire ride. As we glided around the park that night, looking at the winking lights of the Big Apple, I couldn't shake the sinking feeling that Arledge's silent anger meant ESPN's ride with ABC wasn't going to be nearly as smooth as the one around the park.

Despite Arledge's ruthless leadership—or perhaps, to some degree, because of it—ESPN would continue to gather serious attention from the media marketplace and become a sparkling, lucrative gem among the crown jewels of diversified operations at Getty Oil.

In 1984, the potential for an even bigger deal seemed in the offing. In fact, during that time in the inner sanctum of Getty, the place was rife with the prospects that the company might be sold. I was invited to join ABC while I was in Sarajevo, Yugoslavia, for the Winter Olympics. As a group of us rode along in a bus heading for one of the venues, I seated myself next to Fred Pierce and casually broached the question of the sale of the rest of Getty's interest in ESPN. As we headed toward a squeaky stop by the bright, new stadium, I was pleased to hear the somewhat reserved gentleman suggest we get together to revisit the idea before dinner. We sat down later in some overstuffed chairs overlooking the mountain and continued our conversation. I drank ouzo, a strong anisette-flavored liquor of Greece that somehow conjured up my tequila days in Mexico.

"I don't want to be encouraging," Pierce said. "We're cash poor."

I acted surprised.

"We're renegotiating Barbara Walters' contract. Got some other things cooking that will cost us a lot of money. It's probably not a good time for me to float the idea."

I figured he was telling the truth because I had heard about the Barbara Walters negotiation and knew that they had invested heavily in other ventures, including cable programming.

"What is the exact deal?" Pierce asked.

"I'm thinking of $175 million for the remaining 75 percent," I said. "That's a pretty good deal," I hastened to point out.

"Still a lot of money," Pierce said.

"Yes, but ESPN is much bigger and stronger than when you made the original investment for 10 percent in 1982."

At the time, I figured it would have been a good price for us at Getty, should the prospect of someone buying the company become a reality. Also, the cash in the bank would likely be of greater interest to the purchaser than a cable television network that was sucking up $25 million per year.

"I'm just projecting this as a possibility," I told Pierce. "You do have the right of first refusal in our present agreement. If this thing goes into play without me having control of it, it could cost you a lot of money if you want the majority interest in ESPN and are forced to top other offers."

Whether it was because of the network's financial situation or his reservations, Pierce and his ABC network didn't pursue purchasing ESPN. I shook it off, surprised though I was. I figured I might get a call after he had thought about it or consulted some of his management.

But ABC needn't have been out of it yet, for when the announcement came later that year that Getty intended to sell its assets to Texaco—which included ESPN—it kicked in that right of first refusal for ABC to purchase

ESPN from Getty—or Texaco, for that matter—if either elected to sell its interest in ESPN. We had determined in meetings with Texaco that they did not intend to keep ESPN. Quite simply, the petroleum giant had to amass a lot of money to buy Getty, and at a price that would amount to, at the time, the highest corporate purchase in history. Then came the worrisome task of nourishing the company, and ESPN still needed a lot of nourishment in 1984.

Texaco officials asked me if I knew of any interested parties that might want to buy the newly purchased sports operation. "It would be pretty easy to get the word out," I said. "There are some that likely might."

In less than five minutes after I had left, I was sitting in my rental car busily composing a list of some potential players, buyers with the cash and possibly the motivation: Ted Turner, Landmark Communications, as well as several others. Immediately, I thought of my friend Bill Daniels, who was a communications broker. I was consumed with some deals in the agriculture division of Getty and, besides, I didn't want to broker a deal. I would bring in Daniels.

I made an appointment for Daniels and I to meet Texaco's senior management at the company's headquarters in Rye, New York. Daniels did a presentation of what his organization had done in similar situations—and what he could do for Texaco—to effect a sale. The dialogue was direct and flowed quickly over the subject of his brokering the sale.

After Daniels' presentation, I thought it was all a done deal, though not done. But I left there uncertain. There was something unusual, a subtext, perhaps. I couldn't put my finger on it, though. Maybe I was imagining things.

Soon, I learned that, indeed, we were up against an undercurrent of minor intrigue attached to the situation that seemed to be following me everywhere, like a moth fluttering around my head.

I learned that something big was about to unfold in the Texaco Corporation offices. About the time that I was certain the deal had unraveled as completely as a baseball patched up with too much electrical tape, I learned that one of the members of the Texaco board of directors, Tom Murphy, chairman of Capital Cities Corporation, was also a board member of ABC.

The man from Capital Cities, it appeared, was counseling Texaco to negotiate a direct sale to ABC and thus eliminate any possibility of ABC having to top other offers. ABC would then acquire majority interest in ESPN. ABC bought ESPN for a price of $225 million, substantially more than the $175 million price tag I had offered them in Sarajevo.

Pricing is not an easy matter, especially when someone has put a lot of investment dollars into something, as we had in ESPN. But I had laid the groundwork for pricing with the original option price, by which I sold 10 percent to ABC for $20 million. The move served as a guideline toward an attempt to determine a solid value, one that would possibly be within the realm of enticement. It really set the stage for future value.

This earlier purchase-option agreement with ABC also held other benefits. For one thing, it helped me at home with Getty Oil. Not only had the company received a needed infusion of substantial cash to help with operating expenses, I could start using that figure as a kind of baseline for value. Not too bad to be talking about those kinds of numbers when the perceived value at the time among many people, including some of our corporate Getty people, was that no value at all was attached to this lost horizon we called ESPN.

It was as if we had painfully continued to take our medicine over all those years of ownership and, after all this suffering, it had somehow made us better.

I remember sitting down to write what was a difficult, though perhaps simple-enough, letter to the ESPN employees. The letter, dated May 2, 1984, included the following:

> While all of us involved with the development and growth of ESPN since its inception may have mixed and, perhaps, sad feelings in this change of ownership, you can take comfort in the knowledge that your contributions to the dynamic success of ESPN have been confirmed by the monetary magnitude of this sale. The sale of ESPN to ABC represents the largest and most profitable transaction of its kind in cable industry history.

I wanted to thank the people of ESPN. I thought of so many people as I wrote: Bill Grimes, Bill Creasy, Rosa Gatti, Scotty Connal, Jim Simpson, Bob Ley, Roger Werner, George Bodenheimer, Lois Moreno, Jim Dullaghan, Joe Valario, who produces the *Sports Reporters* weekly show for ESPN—and so many others, including Chet Simmons.

I concluded, my face moist with tears:

> During my business career, I have never had the opportunity of associating with people who were more conscientious and dedicated to success. I thank you for giving me that privilege.

Today, the value of ESPN has been estimated at $18 billion. Broadcast success story of the century? Some say so. I guess it depends on which end you find yourself.

I take my credit, but I continue to believe that the success of ESPN, over time, stems from the succession of ownership. Getty, of course, was the first. And Getty wouldn't have gotten into it without me. I am confident that Getty would not have stayed in it for that long without me. But realistically, I don't think Getty could have taken the all-sports network to the level it is today. It wasn't part of our core business, but if the gusher it ultimately became had happened early on, the future for Getty and ESPN may well have been much different.

Furthermore, when ESPN was included in the sale of Getty to Texaco which, in turn, sold it to ABC, ESPN acquired the requisite tough-minded, broadcast mentality. ABC knew what was going on at all times in the sports television business. It wasn't, as it had been with us, a new project every time.

Though ESPN was proving its viability, flack still blossomed in the skies for anyone else who associated with it—including Fred Pierce of ABC, who writes in Goldenson's *Beating the Odds* about how the purchase of ESPN came at the wrong time: a time after high revenues, but a time when demands on money for such things as ARTS and Satellite News Channel had drawn deeply into the corporation's coffers.

In view of flat network revenues, Goldenson writes: "So now here comes Fred and he says, 'Leonard, we are going to buy the rest of ESPN—and by the way, it's losing $25 million a year.'"

The degree of confusion and resentment that surrounded this thing called sports cable can be seen in the following Pierce quote: "When the announcement of our acquisition was made, there was a flood of criticism, not just from our broadcast affiliates. Many said they thought we'd been hornswoggled into buying a pink elephant. Others . . . called me a traitor to network broadcasting. And still others said I'd lost my mind to spend that much money on anything."

So rancorous were attitudes toward cable that one broadcast executive told me that cable was a horrible Orwellian scheme, the wired world of government eavesdropping. "Once they've got the wires in . . ." he said. "Like the telephone?" I said.

When Capital Cities bought ABC in 1985, they introduced chairman Tom Murphy's trademark fiscal responsibility to the combined networks. Limousines, apartments, and airplanes were considered excesses and were no longer common practice. I found this quite interesting because many of these same budgeting, forecasting, and planning procedures were part of the early Getty-ESPN operating environment. Bill Creasy, a veteran NBC producer who produced ESPN's opening show, said, "I always tell people that Getty had the courage and vision to start it, and then they sold it to Texaco. And Texaco sold it to ABC. But it wasn't until Capital Cities got involved, along with Chairman Tom Murphy, that it really got going. They had considerable vision and, most importantly, the deep pockets too."

In 1996, the Disney-Capital Cities/ABC merger created even greater opportunities for ESPN. Cross promotions, ownership of professional sports teams, and the opportunity to introduce the entertainment part of ESPN's name became realities. Movies, reality shows, and other expanded proprietary programming are now prominent in ESPN's schedule. It wasn't long before other giant corporations and conglomerates moved heavily into the field of broadcasting. In fact, I had often predicted that the rapidly changing economics of broadcasting would attract major corporations. Though often maligned by media critics, it seemed clear to me that the broadcast model couldn't continue as it had in the past. Westinghouse and General Electric bought CBS and NBC. Now, large corporate entities own television networks.

At the risk of letting my ego climb back in the saddle and whip the horse, I must take credit for the movement toward major corporation ownership because we at Getty got it all started—despite the fact that big mergers are often pooh-poohed by the media and popular sentiment, which doesn't bother me. Certainly there are good mergers and bad ones, but the concept is not bad, and it often, as in the case of ESPN, helps move an entity to a higher level.

Finally, I take some pride in the fact that we at Getty helped to introduce a stronger, more consistent business model into the broadcast and communications mix through implementations in budgeting and other monetary restraints.

CHAPTER 15

THE PIED PIPER OF ESPN

Of the people responsible for hiring our staff in the beginning of ESPN, I would have to say that Scotty Connal, along with Jim Simpson, were keys to our early success. Connal made things happen, selected a lot of good young people, drew a large number of professionals from NBC, imparted distinctive innovation, and established the kind of atmosphere and professionalism that a start-up operation consisting mostly of beginners must have to endure.

Connal was one thing, but along with his wife, Till (for Mathilde), they were an employer's dream. Before their marriage, they had started their careers at NBC—Till in 1946, Scotty a year later. Till was a switchboard operator and met Scotty through her brother, who asked her to take care of his friend, Scotty, who had recently gone to work as a page at NBC. At the time, NBC was in a closet on the fourth floor and featured the Blue and Red networks.

Scotty Connal went from NBC page to vice president, and at every step along the way, Till says he "learned an awful lot." He lived most of his life in Yonkers, New York, was educated at Roosevelt High School, and then took various college courses. Till offered a little play on words when discussing his formal education: "Rather than a full degree, he had a degree in this and a degree in that."

In 1979, Connal agreed to join ESPN. Soon thereafter, word reached NBC management that he was planning to join ESPN. While he was broadcasting the All-Star Game, the Nationals won in Seattle, Robert Wussler, then-president of NBC Sports, ambled up to Till, cornering her on a bench. He looked as if he had received a full slap of reality. Wussler said in his slangy voice, "Till, what can I do to keep Scotty?"

Till said, "That's not a discussion you have with me. That's a discussion you have with Scotty. That's entirely his decision."

Wussler said, "Well, he can write his own ticket."

Till was surprised. "I thought that was interesting," she reflected later. She knew her husband had a mind of his own. Before long, Connal took the job with ESPN and moved into the Farmington Inn, his home for the next six months, before his family moved to Bristol. Connal, a 22-year veteran of broadcasting, began a new life in a business that was frighteningly groundbreaking, but in his mind, it represented the future of sports television.

Scotty Connal's penchant for detail, as well as his knowledge of things technical, proved invaluable in those early years at ESPN. Even in the first year, he frequently had to marshal, as efficiently as a veteran travel agent, broadcast and technical crews across the country, matching skills with the necessities of production. He managed persons and equipment for nearly one hundred basketball games that year. Furthermore, that was the year that the network began to broadcast early games in the NCAA tournament, with Jim Simpson at the mike—a shifting coverage that has electrified basketball fans since and, quite possibly, has helped to make the NCAA tournament the center of attention it is today. Dan Fitzgerald, the legendary coach of the Gonzaga Bulldogs, later told me, "ESPN was the single most important factor for the popularity of college basketball."

Connal met with some discouraging comments, bordering on insults, like the rest of us in those days. After a short time, according to his wife, he began to call all his friends in television and relate to them what he intended to do. Many insistently reminded him of the practicalities—even realities—of the industry. The conversations troubled him. He was calling his friends for a certain kind of confirmation and, for the most part, he didn't get it, even from colleagues and friends who usually supported him.

Connal wasn't altogether pleased with the deadline for the opening show, but he knew how to react under pressure. "They want to go on the air in September," he had told some during his calls. "There's nothing there, no studios, and minimal broadcast facilities." But Connal was determined and had come to stay. He would make it work; he read everything he could on satellite communication. He studied into the night, and he and the others would solve the damnably nettling technical problems that cropped up like spats in an iffy relationship.

There was nothing hard-edged about Scotty. He had a mellow personality and was, more or less, easy-going with a shy, deferential manner. He only became perturbed when the technical lid blew off the place. He was the opposite of Chet Simmons that way.

Connal shouldered the burden during some crucial times, even when he wasn't on the premises. I noticed at social gatherings, even large and boisterous ones, that he always had his eye on the television, watching ESPN, ready at any moment to call in corrections or critique the broadcast. Likely the most famous—or infamous—example was the *Heidi* game when he was working at NBC Sports. The incident involved the network cutting away from the Oakland Raiders–New York Jets NFL game prematurely to begin the children's film *Heidi*. At the time, the incident stood out as a kind of in-your-face affront to almost every sports fan who witnessed it, and perhaps to just as many who didn't. And Connal, though he was not working and was at home watching the game, nearly managed to avert the calamity. He called in and tried to convince the technicians on duty not to go to the film, but he wasn't able to get through in time. As he was calling, the bright and happy opening of *Heidi* burst forth like a horrible, badly timed jester. The upshot was that the viewing public missed the Raiders electrifying 43–32 comeback win, and for some time, letters decried the incident, which, in turn, gave pundits and columnists plenty of fodder.

At his core, Connal was the kind of person who believed in people. I used to think of Scotty Connal as the "Pied Piper of ESPN" because of his active support and ongoing encouragement of a whole new group of young, ambitious media minds. When ESPN was started, word spread rapidly about the operation. Unlike the traditional networks, ESPN was to be nonunion. This gave new employees the opportunity to apply their skills and aspirations to every facet of the broadcasting business. Hundreds of young people interested in television, or those who generally loved sports, came calling or sent résumés. Scotty and Till Connal assiduously sorted through filled apple cartons, evaluating each résumé. A certain number of young people were hired, and many of them had, to that point, little or no experience in television or cable, but that did not matter. Connal turned them into professionals. He took interest in them; he supported them. In most instances, he turned them from wide-eyed novices to broadcast professionals.

Connal had an eye for talent. Take George Bodenheimer, for example. Connal had taught Bodenheimer hockey as a kid. One day, Connal came home and mentioned Bodenheimer to Till over dinner, "You know George Bodenheimer just started working at ESPN. He's such a fine young man. He's going to go far."

When Bodenheimer was made president of ESPN after Connal's death, Till wrote Bodenheimer a letter saying, "George, guess what? Scotty knew you were going to go far."

Connal also deserves credit for hiring Dick Vitale and Chris Berman, two of ESPN's most distinctive television mainstays.

The Connals also helped to build a community of ESPN folks. They bought a large comfortable house on Cedar Lake in Bristol and frequently invited the ESPN staff for parties and gatherings. Anywhere from 20 to 40 people would show up, whether it was for a picnic or a more formal sit-down dinner. The Connals usually invited the engineering and production teams separately.

In essence, the Connals—Scotty, Till, and the rest of their family—established a comfortable little respite for the ESPNers, a home away from home for many people who might otherwise have felt disenfranchised having come to a small, new place and to a radically new type of job.

Reports of sexual harassment, drug abuse, and out-of-control behavior have been played up greatly in at least one other book about ESPN, and the accounts have, unfortunately, taken on lives of their own and have threatened to diminish—or at least overshadow—what everyone accomplished at ESPN in those early days. Excesses happen, but I do not believe the corporate environment sanctioned or turned a blind eye to them in any way. The year 1979 marked the beginning of a period when women began to move aggressively into different roles and venues, and sometimes the treatment they received was less civil, decent, and respectful than it should have been. Other times, hormones and appetites no doubt raged. While any harassment that truly happened should not be dismissed, it also is wrong, distasteful, and distorted to focus on them. They were not central to the operation, and they certainly were not allowed to denigrate either the professionalism Connal championed or the standards he set. He simply would not countenance any tendency toward disgrace.

Beyond the staffing, production, and programming duties, Connal belonged in the world of sports. He loved it, especially hockey. He had a real reputation as not only a skater, but also a hockey player. His wife, Till, recalls his stint in the army. He made sure to pack his ice skates for his time in Mannheim, Germany. He found the time to visit the local rink, and eventually met and skated with the German hockey team. With the U.S. Army's explicit sanction, which zealously sought to build a productive American-German relationship, Connal became a sort of goodwill ambassador during post-war reconstruction and the Cold War.

When ESPN moved into hockey, it was Connal who moved it there. It was his knowledge and appreciation of the game that made the difference. Who says one's vocation and avocation can't come together? (Yes, it was Robert Frost, I know.) In hockey, as with other aspects, Connal was persistent and dedicated. Every detail had to be right. He had to see things through to the end. Ted Lindsey, a close friend who played in the NHL for the Detroit Red Wings, remembers, "There was hardly anyone ever unhappy with him. Everybody had a job to do, and if Scotty wanted them to work for 36 hours, they worked 36 hours. And that's a gift he had as a leader."

Lindsey adds: "He respected your talents, and he respected your abilities, and he let you do everything. At our meetings, he never really dictated anything. He let you do your job. He wanted everyone to realize he was not a boss; he was not an authority—he was a friend. I think when a person with authority can convey that message, it breeds success."

Connal's knowledge of hockey resulted in his going to Canada to help them refine their techniques in broadcasting the games on television. Ralph Mellanby of the Canadian Broadcasting Corporation, is unequivocal when he says, "Scotty taught us how to televise hockey."

Although Scotty Connal was never able to get big-time hockey going at NBC during his time there, he still had the courage and persistence to introduce it in grand style at ESPN. At ESPN, hockey became a success, and one more rung on the ladder of acquiring the rights to broadcast live professional sports.

Ralph Mellanby also remembers the vision that Connal had for ESPN: "He once told me, 'I'm going to be able to do something I've never done before as an executive producer.' I expressed my doubts, and then he said, 'We'll do lots of things. We'll even repeat stuff. It's cable, so people can't see it all at the same time. At three in the morning, we'll repeat the NIT basketball game.' I said, 'That might work.' But essentially, Scotty had a feel for and a belief in ESPN from the start."

At the end of Chet Simmons' reign at ESPN, the goodwill apparently slipped from his and Scotty's relationship. Chet never really supported Scotty for advancement to president, nor did he give him a reason for not doing so, despite a long and winding past together. To this day, the tension over the fallout among the Connals persists. Connal's son, Bruce, a producer who works for ESPN as a contractor on hockey, said, "My father continually supported Chet for years and years and would always do things that would elevate Chet, and yet Chet never really reciprocated." The slights obviously weighed on Connal. "Scotty never really talked about it [not getting the top job]," said Till, "but he obviously was a little let down. I was probably more upset because I was close and knew a lot about the history of their relationship. But Scotty said, 'No, that's the way it is. That's the way it is. If that's what they want, let them do it.'" Connal, who served as a key figure during Simmons' tenure—and afterward—and who had exerted a steadying, tempering force on Simmons' sometimes abrasive personality, was himself treated abrasively in the end.

Connal believed in the possibility of ESPN, and he surely deserves his due, for he never really received it. I last saw him in New York after he left ESPN. He had not changed, nor had I expected him to.

He died just a week after his birthday, when he suffered an aneurysm while staying in Atlanta, Georgia, working at the Olympics. His memorial service had an incredible attendance. The crew went to the memorial service and stood in the hall crying afterward. They had what is called a "run-up" scheduled before the last volleyball game to be played in the series. A run-up is where a lead-in to the game is produced, and a few details are hashed out. They had an identifier, a volleyball that they recorded, and superimposed on it was the information identifying the venue. On the volleyball in Magic Marker, the production crew had written: "Good-bye, Scotty."

Scotty Connal actually had two funerals: the first in Atlanta and another in Greenwich, Connecticut. After the first funeral, Connal's wife was confronted by hometown friends who insisted that Connal be remembered there, as well. They said, "You can't leave it there. You have to have it here. There are too many people who want to say good-bye." Three hundred people went to his funeral in Atlanta; two hundred and fifty more paid their last respects to Connal in Greenwich.

So many people wanted to say good-bye. Millions had watched his innovations in sports: coloring the ice blue for hockey games, putting microphones in the holes at golf matches, or his favorite camera shot, the one that worked so beautifully when Carleton Fisk "pushed" his game-winning homer fair in the sixth game of the 1975 World Series (a broadcast that won Connal an Emmy). He also helped to refine slow-motion techniques with storage on a 24" disc that enabled easy transition from slow motion back to live action. Few viewers would appreciate the influence Scotty Connal had on sports television, but his legacy is felt by us all, especially at ESPN.

These days, I think of Connal and I think of sports: his infectious love of sports, which so mirrored mine. I see ESPN, and I think of Connal. I'd like to be able to sit down for a refreshment at the Bull and the Bear at the Waldorf Astoria, or some small bar or restaurant in Bristol, or somewhere in between, and talk with him again about this year's Stanley Cup. He was always a winner.

CHAPTER 16

ESPN's Golden Throat

I always thought Jim Simpson was one of the most important people hired at ESPN. The following is a conversation that my associate, Irv Broughton, had with Simpson. This informal discussion shows the kind of person Simpson really is—the consummate broadcast sports professional who set the tone and the standard for future television sportscasters at ESPN and elsewhere.

In a career of close to 50 years, Simpson has shown a versatility and talent virtually unmatched in sports broadcasting. Name a major sporting event, and Simpson has been at the microphone: the 1964 Summer Olympics, the first *Wide World of Sports*, NFL on NBC, the Super Bowl, the Orange Bowl, the Davis Cup and Grand Slam tennis, the Major League All-Star Game, the Wimbledon Championship, and the World Series. He has broadcast in 50 states and the District of Columbia, as well as 29 countries. At ESPN, which he joined in 1979, Simpson covered the USFL; college baseball, football and basketball; boxing; golf; horse racing; and tennis—most notably the Davis Cup. He even did some duty anchoring ESPN's *SportsCenter* in 1979. Fittingly, before he came to the satellite world of ESPN, he had made history as the first sports broadcaster to appear via satellite from Asia during the 1964 Summer Olympics.

Simpson's numerous awards include the College Sports Information Directors of America (CoSIDA) Jake Wade Award in 1994, and the Lifetime Achievement Award from the Academy of Television Arts and Sciences. He is a member of the National Sportscasters and Sportswriters Association of America Hall of Fame.

Irv Broughton: You were a mentor of the younger people at ESPN during the early days.

Jim Simpson: It was exciting to do. It was different to do at that time because we had a lot of kids right out of school, and they had never had really done anything like this before. I became, in the minds of many, a taskmaster. The fact that ESPN was launched as a nonunion network, the opportunities for these multitalented young professionals were significant. They could perform most any task, from writing script, to pulling cable, to operating booms and cameras, without the restrictions imposed by a union shop. That made ESPN a haven for wannabes, because [such experience] was not available at any of the major networks. A few years later I went back to Bristol to play in the Rotary [Club Annual] Golf Tournament that ESPN sponsored. I saw many who had been with me in the beginning: Steve Hanson, John Wilde, and George Bodenheimer, who had started his career in the mailroom and later became president of ESPN! Each one thanked me for the direction and time I'd given them. But I used to be tough on the young people. What is significant is that I was used to tough standards of broadcasting, and ESPN didn't have any standards at that time.

Broughton: You began at WTOP as a sports anchor.

Simpson: I'd been in radio before that. I first found WOIC, which was Channel 9 in Washington, and started in January 1948.

It became WTOP. At any rate, I had the top-rated local show for the two years I was the local anchor—with Walter Cronkite. We had the *Cronkite-Simpson Report*. I think there were five thousand television sets in the whole city at that time. But we had the top show.

Broughton: Any good stories about working with Cronkite?

Simpson: Not really, except one time he said if a couple of guys and I came out to paint the fence at his new home, he'd provide the "liquid refreshment," which was so refreshing that he threw us out of his yard and wouldn't speak to us again for several days. "Hide the Heineken! Simpson's coming home!"

Of course, nobody knew that Walter Cronkite would become the legend he became or that I would go on in the field of sports-casting like I did.

In 1955, I went over to WRC, Channel 4, where they had a local weatherman in Willard Scott, and [a puppet named] Sam used to lip-sync Spike Jones numbers—passionate love songs—to his friends. Later, Jim Henson and his girlfriend [later his wife], Jane Nebel, changed Sam's name to Kermit, and you know the rest. Our NBC Christmas parties featuring Willard Scott as Santa Claus became the Muppets. At the NBC Christmas party, Willard Scott was Santa Claus, and the very early Muppets were the enter-tainment. After them, I coanchored the news with Walter Cronkite. Those days were exciting.

Broughton: Television was primitive when you started out in TV sports.

Simpson: Oh yes. We had no teleprompters, and I was too damn blind to see the cue cards across the way and probably too damn lazy to use them. For that reason, I used to write with big letters with numbers on sheets of paper. I could do a 10-minute sports show without using a script or looking down at the numbers. My memory was good because it was just organized to do that. I would give the control room a name, like Stu Evey, and say, "When you hear that name, wave and say, "Five, four, three, two, one second." One time, the guy in the control room wasn't listening, and I repeated myself, I said, "Stu Evey," hoping to loosen them up in the control room so they could roll the film. I said "Stu" again when the director finally woke up. The film rolled, and the show was about over—with one story!

It was pretty basic. NBC owned WRC at the time and still does. Once we were supposed to be covering important [Washington] Redskins trade news, but there was a fire in a tire place in suburban Virginia, and all the tires caught on fire. This was great footage for the news anchor, so away went my film cameraman to watch the fire drill. I had three-and-half minutes, which was all they gave you in those days in a half-hour show. As a result of the fire, they cut my segment on a big trade announcement by the city's beloved Redskins down to a one-and-a-half-minute segment. They figured I was ad-libbing and could get out of there easily enough. Later, I went down to the producer, and I said, "I can tell you why there's a hunger strike in Gdansk, Poland, if you can tell me who the Redskins are playing next week." I got him on that. I said, "You've got to know everything. It would be good if the president of NBC had the sports section on his desk every day, and it wouldn't be long before he asked, 'Where's the sports section?' and then buzzed for his secretary." I said, "Sports are very important to people. You think they're not important. They're only two to three minutes." I'm not so sure the news producer took me to heart. But he *depended* on me in my ad-libbing of sports events. If a news segment ran over, or the producer needed more time, he would "cut" me right in the middle of my camera work, knowing I could and would exit in a hurry.

Broughton: Are you a gambler by nature?

Simpson: My wife loves the slots, but I'd rather save the money and take you out to lunch.

Broughton: I'll take you up on that.

Simpson: I gambled on ESPN only because of Evey, only because he called me five nights a week for damn near a year before I went with him. He's convincing. But that was just a heck of a sales job—but I'm glad I bought it.

Broughton: What do you recall about those dialogues?

Simpson: I could not visualize, in 1979, cable becoming what it has become in 2004. To me, cable was mom-and-pop operations in the hinterland. Stu sent me all kinds of articles of where cable was going—and how it was going to grow. He sent me information about what Getty Oil Company was, for heaven's sake. I knew it was Getty Oil, but at first, I didn't know what they were doing and what Stu's position was. At the time I didn't know he was standing behind the biggest gamble of his business career. He had put a very successful career at Getty on the line.

Broughton: What did you think when you met Stu?

Simpson: I didn't know what to think. I was literally in awe of the guy who had put that kind of money at risk when I didn't even know that cable had the possibility or probability of succeeding. It reminded me of the night when I was finished with a segment of the *Cronkite-Simpson Report* on Channel 9, the producer of the half-hour talk show pulled me from the studio. Because of the blinding snowstorm outside, the host of the talk show was stuck at home. Only one of three scheduled guests had made it to the station. I would have to go down the hall to another studio and handle the half hour. The guest was there to talk of space travel. I can't remember whether he was a part of NASA or even if the agency was called NASA in 1951. I performed a rare feat for me: I kept my mouth immobile for nearly the whole half hour. The much older scientist—he must have been at least 45—was fascinating. At the half hour's conclusion, I asked something like, "Professor, are you telling me that in my lifetime someone will walk on the moon?" The guest looked intently and sincerely at me and replied, "Young man, someone will walk on the moon in my lifetime!" Show over. "Space man" exited into the thick snow. I, the director, and all the CBS engineers were all of the same thought: "The man is crazy. Walk on the moon? And [to] come out in this snow storm to be on this show proves he's crazy!" He wasn't, of course. Man landed and walked on the moon less than 20 years after that show in a snowstorm. And I remembered my disbelief of the future of space travel when Stu kept calling. Was Stu crazy? Or could he envision the future clearer than I?

Broughton: Describe what Stu Evey looked like back then.

Simpson: He was the man from Getty. He was very frank and very outgoing. There was no formal greeting. He was a very informal person. At least, he was with me.

It was an amicable meeting and has been for almost 25 years now.

Broughton: Were you ever frightened about your decision to go to ESPN?

Simpson: My decision was not a gamble, and I've said this too often. We had a nephew living in our house. There were eight of us living there, as well as a dog and two pussycats. The other two kids were in college.

Broughton: Stu indicated that an inducement to signing you was that your wife, Sara, could travel with you.

Simpson: Sara had to pick her spots traveling with me, leaving the gang behind. She opted for the Olympic Games, the Bob Hope Classic, and she loved Wimbledon. With precious little free time, she had to be choosy. When I started working with ESPN and was on the road, she went everywhere! A basketball game here tonight, a show in Bristol tomorrow, another game the next night. Packing and unpacking daily brought the comment, "This is tough. This is living out of a bag."

Broughton: How many days did you go out a year?

Simpson: We logged about 280 days for three or four years.

Broughton: And you did everything.

Simpson: We covered everything. At NBC, I had covered major sporting events—collegiate football, NFL, basketball's Final Four, Wimbledon tennis—everything. At ABC, I was doing events that had never been televised before. At ESPN, what was available was what we did. I was fortunate. Most sportscasters today are hired for a single specialty or show, maybe. I got to do it all! I've been asked, "What was your favorite?" I always answer, "I put myself in competition with myself at every event. Be better today than you were yesterday, and tomorrow, do better than today, and better than that the day after tomorrow."

For NBC, I was assigned the backup Major League game of the week seen in those two markets where the teams comprised the national telecast. If there was rain in the national market, our backup game would be national. One analyst, hearing there was a likelihood of going national, began to sweat because of the pressure of being heard everywhere. I told him, "I don't think you tried less hard when only two thousand watched your game, and then tried harder when twenty thousand watched. Give it your best shot every time!"

Broughton: What did you think when you first saw Bristol?

Simpson: I never saw Bristol. I saw ESPN and the one building they had because they drove me right to the airport and right past Bristol. It's like in Carolina. If you're recruiting, you take the recruit and drive them over the railroad tracks first to North Carolina State and then take them to the beautiful Duke campus. They didn't let me see Bristol—not that Bristol was bad, don't get me wrong. I just saw the inside of a motel—I've forgotten which—and the studio, which was nothing but concrete with flies all over. Still, it was exciting because I got back to the idea of going to the moon and I met some neat people there. But you knew it was a start-up operation.

Broughton: How do you remember Chet Simmons?

Simpson: He'd criticize the hell out of you. He would almost put your career on the line, but if someone else from outside ESPN criticized you, he would be your watchdog and protect you. He was a tough taskmaster. Maybe some of that wore off on me. Also, Chet knew how to handle negotiations. He knew how to get the most out of people.

Broughton: What was your favorite ESPN broadcast?

Simpson: I'd like to say my first, which was the Iowa–Nebraska football game. I showed up in Cedar Rapids, Iowa, and went down to Iowa City to a press conference. There was also a press party that night. When I got back to the hotel in Cedar

Rapids, I called Scotty Connal, my executive producer at ESPN, and said, "Where is everybody?" He said, "What do you mean 'everybody?'" I said, "There's not a director, producer, remote unit—anything—here. I am it."

The next morning, I went back to Iowa City and found the cameras had been set up and the remote unit had arrived. We did an amazing game, which was decided at the last moment. One of the Nebraska coaches came up to me and said, "When will it be broadcast?" It was on tape. And I said, "I don't know, but give me your address and phone and I'll let you know." The coach said, "I want all my possible recruits to see Nebraska play football. I'm going to call them and tell them when to watch." Now that was memorable."

Other favorites include the McEnroe–Wilander match at the Davis Cup in St. Louis. There were no tie-breakers in Davis Cup play. The final match of the day was between Mats Wilander of Sweden and America's John McEnroe. Stu was in attendance, but had to leave after the first set, for he had an appointment in New York the next morning. Stu was driven to the Getty plane at Lambert Field, flew to LaGuardia, was driven into town, checked into his hotel, and turned on the TV. The local sports anchor did *not* report the result of the Wilander–McEnroe match! Anxiously, Stu called the broadcast center in Bristol and was told the match was still going on. It lasted over five and a half hours. McEnroe, the U.S.A., the winner!

Broughton: Describe the difference between your office at NBC and your office at ESPN.

Simpson: [laughing] I had no office at ESPN. I'd borrow a table or desk if I could. I was only at ESPN to do a show on football. Then I was gone on the road. My office was a motel or hotel room.

Broughton: Most important broadcasts?

Simpson: I think we made the Davis Cup for those who watch tennis. We had an influence on college basketball by doing the preliminary games up to the Final Four. We did the PGA tournament. We did the Thursday and Friday of the PGA and the British Open, as a result of Stu's negotiating a minority sale of ESPN stock to ABC, who held the rights to these major golf events. I was out in the cornfield in the British Open. They had built a platform for me and about 50 yards from me was the North Sea. The wind was coming off that chilling, forbidding sea, blowing the cold into my shaking body—and I had four more hours to go! I watched a commercial appear on the monitor and said to our talented producer, Bill Fitts, "If you don't get me off this platform, I'll be one stick of ice, and you'll have to scrape me off." About 30 minutes later, during another commercial, I ran into the caravan of trailers, where Bill was in charge of coverage, and they'd rehooked things up, and I did the sportscast from there.

Broughton: You worked with Bud Wilkinson. How did that happen?

Simpson: I'd known Bud for some years. We had done the Orange Bowl game when Joe Namath, after Texas edged his favored Alabama team, began a new era of pro football—and a $400,000 contract with the New York Jets. I had done Oklahoma games when Bud was its outstanding coach, and he moved to the Washington area, where I lived, to chair the President's Council on Physical Fitness. After Bud was fired as head coach of the NFL St. Louis Cardinals, Chet Simmons called me and said, "Maybe you could get Bud to work with you." So I called him, but he seemed reluctant at first. I said, "I don't know how much they'll be willing to pay at ESPN, or if they'll pay. But," I said, "I know you and I will have fun." Bud said, "Let's do it!"

I remember the first time ESPN was doing an Oklahoma game in Norman, Oklahoma, I looked up and saw this great, big sports complex with Bud's name on it. I said, "Mr. Wilkinson, you never told me about that." He said, "That was nice of them, wasn't it?" He was a genuinely modest man.

Broughton: Did you broadcast the first game with Dick Vitale?

Simpson: No, not the first, but one day Scotty Connal called me in and said that Dick, who had been fired as coach of the Detroit Pistons and was now working for ESPN, was walking all over everybody on the air—interrupting everyone. Scotty said, "If you can't work with him, we'll have to let him go." I was sent out to Chicago to do a DePaul basketball game with Dick. When I arrived, I told our producer, Bobby Feller, that if Dick steps all over me when I'm speaking, then I'm going to ask you to cut Dick's mike. Bobby said OK. Because it was a late game, we went to dinner first, and during dinner, Dick started in. He said, "You're this and that. You're a sports legend." I said, "Well, Dick, if you don't stop what you're saying to everyone you see, I'm going to tell Scotty not to keep you." He said, "What am I saying?" I said, "You're saying, 'I'm a bald, one-eyed, fired coach.' I'm sorry you're bald, I'm sorry that you had a childhood accident with your eye, and name a coach besides John Wooden who has not been fired. You're here as the integrity of ESPN basketball, and get off that personal stuff. Get on with the game." So the game began, and DePaul ran out to a 10-point lead, so the other team called a time-out. During the time-out, I said to Bobby, "Cut Dick's microphone," which he did. At that, Dick's face went pale as a sheet. One of the teams called time-out a couple of minutes later, and I turned to Dick and said, "Are you ready now?" He said, "Being a good coach, I like to be coached." I said, "You know my cadence. You know what I'm doing. You should know when to interject comments into the play-by-play." Bobby turned his mike back on, and, guess what, he was perfect from then on. Now he's a total pro and rightfully nominated for the Broadcasters Hall of Fame.

Broughton: One of the strangest situations you broadcast?

Simpson: I was broadcasting the 1952 Olympics in Helsinki on radio. I watched as Pavo Nurmi, the country's greatest distance runner, brought in the Olympic torch. The "March In" of athletes took my breath away. Suddenly, as the athletes were marching out onto the field, this woman suddenly appeared in long, white robes. I thought she was part of the ceremony, a sign of Peace in the World, I wondered out loud. Eero [Lesio], my interpreter next to me, said, "She's crazy." He was looking through binoculars to the other side of the field. I wondered how he had known that when she was so far away. I said, "No, she's not nuts." Then officials began to mount the stairs behind her, but the "Woman in White" beat them to the microphone. In calm, but passionate tones, she began to plea for freedom for her Balkan homeland dominated by the Soviets. I think security first thought the same as I, that she was an athlete, but when they realized differently, they wrapped her up and carried her away.

Broughton: Ever get so wrapped up in a sporting event that you almost can't speak?

Simpson: That's what you're looking forward to. That's what you really are waiting for. If I did a 75–0 football game, I wouldn't hear a comment about my performance, even though it might have been my best job ever. But if I did a game won by a field goal in the last two seconds where I may have made eight mistakes, I'd hear, "You were great." To that, I'd say, "No, the game was great!" It was funny. The closer the game got, the more excited I'd become—not on air, necessarily, but within myself. I'd think, I've got something here with which to work.

Broughton: Did Scotty Connal invent the instant replay?

Simpson: We were on the way to the Army–Navy game about 1963, driving in a cab, not a limousine, when our director, Tony Verna, leaned back and said to Lindsey Nelson, "Lindsey, we're going to show a play again." Lindsey said, "How will people know it's not what's going on now?" Tony said, "You're going to have to be very careful about that and tell them. Just tell them more than once." Well, that was the beginning of the instant replay. In the early 1990s, I did the Friendship Games in Tacoma, Washington. Tony Verna was there, and he told me, "There are about 575 people who said they were there when the instant replay happened." The fact: there were just four of us.

Broughton: You grew in stature right along with ESPN.

Simpson: In a lot of my speeches, I tell a story of the day when I finally decided to go to work for ESPN. I drove to the National Airport and found the public parking was all taken. As a consequence, I parked a ways out and climbed into a little, white bus. We were all sitting up straight, and a guy got in with a white jacket with a St. Elizabeth's insignia on the front. He counted, "One, two, three, four, five . . ." and, when he got to me, he said, "Who are you?" I said, "I'm leaving NBC, where I broadcast the Super Bowl, the Orange and Rose Bowls, and Wimbledon tennis, and I'm going to Bristol, Connecticut," and he pointed to me and said, without hesitating, "*six*, seven, eight, nine. . . ."

One time, I was doing a Washington Redskins game. I took my kids and walked into the stadium, and everyone was asking for my autograph. Pretty soon, the players came up and people started to peel off from me and get the players' autographs. Just then, my nine-year-old daughter, B. J., said, "Dad, who did they think you were?" I said, "I can't complain at all. Whoever I am, it's been a wonderful life."

CHAPTER 17

FROM "WHO'S WHO"
TO "WHO'S HE?"

In 1984, with ESPN sold, the phones suddenly stopped ringing. The power lunches belonged at someone else's nice table, and even though those experiences had come to be commonplace, I missed them. I had trouble realizing that what I had done would go on quite well without me. And I was unprepared. Even though I had a year-and-a-half "sabbatical" to prepare for this time, I think time caught up with me. For one thing, it had taken that long for things to settle down, and furthermore, I was not accustomed to stepping away from something. I was conditioned my whole life to forge and charge ahead.

So it came as little surprise that this extra time on my hands became a burden. My relationship with my first wife had suffered—or more accurately—begun to fail, and the more time we had together, the more the problems compounded. Now there seemed little chance we could reconcile. I began to believe that, for years, I had lived behind a wall that protected me from my emotions, but the wall was down, lying there before me, a pile of rubble. About this time, I thought a trip to Europe would suffice as a graceful sanitarium and allow me to think and perhaps recover something. I was gone for two months, much of which I spent in Switzerland, skiing.

But none of my travels, the high life and airy freedom and the heady, brisk atmosphere of the Alps, helped me. I was abject, down, depressed, drinking—and then I wrote a letter to Bill Daniels, head of Daniels Communications in Denver, Colorado. Daniels was a pioneer in cable telecasting and a good friend. I had arranged for him to join the board of H. F. Ahmanson Company, parent of Home Savings of America. We had come to know each other well since our lives crossed in our two telecommunications organizations. In cable, Daniels was big. But now, he was down. I had heard that some of his colleagues had intervened to get him into the Betty Ford Center.

Daniels' reply, sitting there on the dining room table when I came home after a day of drinking, was a distinct echo of myself: "Stu, I am so happy that I'm here at the Ford Center. I never would've come on my own. You know, I'm beginning to learn a little bit about my behavior and about my character and things like that."

I was touched by the letter and went down to visit him in Palm Desert, California. I was emotionally bankrupt: I needed to do something. I had known for some time that alcohol had the huge potential to get me into a lot of trouble. But for the most part, I'd been able to dodge the lethal bullets of booze. Some incidences that combined my imposing ego with demon alcohol were just too close for comfort. To illustrate, I remember vividly a volatile encounter with another towering narcissist.

The year was 1982—a year of conflict, pain, and confusion. I received an invitation by Playboy Enterprises, Inc., founder Hugh Hefner to the Playboy Mansion in Los Angeles, California. Playboy had announced its new cable channel, and Hefner was hosting a gala affair for the members of the National Cable Television Association meeting in Anaheim, California. I decided I would invite my daughter, Christine, to join my then-wife, Shirley, for the event. Christine was, at the time, working in

Hollywood as a gaffer on low-budget films. I thought she might make some connections among the Hollywood crowd we might find at the Mansion. At the outset of the party, I think I stood and watched, a grounded ship with no particular urgencies than to preserve my integrity. Then I loosened up, but not too much.

The evening went wonderfully. I danced the night away with Shirley and Christine, and before the evening ended, I even shared a dance or two with a couple of Playboy bunnies, whose names—but not figures—now escape me. At some point, Heff spoke to us and introduced some lovelies, and then we all returned to dance and drink. While I had been to a large number of major spectacles of American pop culture, notably in the sports arena, this one was the World Series and the All-Star Game all in one—even though there was no score, and there were no hits—at least on my part.

As soon as the party died down some (and apparently Hefner's parties don't really die down: they just enter other days, weeks), I must have decided that my heart or psyche couldn't take it and that we had better call it an evening. The three of us wandered out of the glitter of the immense ballroom to the front of the Mansion. I signaled for a valet when, out of the corner of my eye, I saw someone whom I thought I recognized. I turned to see the visage I hadn't noticed all evening and, if I had, probably would have avoided. It was Ted Turner of Cable News Network (CNN). At his side undulated a statuesque brunette, young and beautiful, many years his junior. I nodded to him.

He turned and walked to within spitting distance of us.

My daughter was closest, so I introduced her first.

"Ted, I'd like you to meet my daughter, Christine," I said, with fatherly pride. Christine is tall and looked as much like a model as his friend did.

"Sure. That's what you say," Turner said, coyly, in his signature rasp. "And I'd like you to meet Tina—*my* daughter."

I was stunned at his comment, his insinuation.

I wish I had decided to sharpen my wit on him because a fight is neither what I wanted nor intended, but I suddenly found myself over-whelmed with anger. I don't know exactly why. Maybe I had the rankling impression that he was cheapening my relationship. Here I was married, with my wife and daughter there—he knew it—and yet he was ridiculing me. Anyway, something just went haywire within me.

Turner was single and with a beautiful girl; there I was, married, and with my beautiful daughter. I'm no prude, though I think I felt like I was being pulled down to his level—or worse. Or maybe I was making a mountain out of a molehill.

I grabbed Turner by the lapels of his sport coat and started a round-house right that might have put me in the cube house of a jail. Fortunately, before I started with a vengeance for his jaw, someone grabbed me hard with both arms from behind. "Better not," the voice yelled out. I usually didn't pay attention to the words "better not," but this time I was pinned. Several partygoers quickly stepped in to fully separate the furious two of us from what might have been an extremely costly exchange of fisted salvos, however sweetly those of mine might have landed on a deserving jaw.

I was wrong, but I also know (or feel strongly) that Ted Turner's atti-tude toward me stemmed to a great extent from past history. He had lost the USFL contract to ESPN and, earlier, I had repelled his interest in merging ESPN and CNN. I can reasonably surmise that all this stuck in his craw and was possibly exacerbated by a few too many drinks that amplified his feelings.

And, of course, egos are not always rational. Maybe the fact that I had a beautiful woman on my arm bothered him, yet this particular corner of the world was so blessed with beauties. Or maybe it was that two recalcitrant, type-A power brokers, with a load of testosterone, had chanced to meet on a field perfect for contest and conquest, and he felt his turf could be yielded only to Mr. Hefner. The two, then, were the only ones entitled to divide the spoils.

I don't believe in settling things with fists, but the confrontation affected me, and Turner probably felt the same. Maybe I had an inkling that I would have to deal with the problem of alcohol, which had become too large a part of a life—a life that seemed to be growing smaller.

Without an effort like an ESPN or Sutton Place or Premiere to keep me charged and motivated, I could feel myself slipping further and further. Nothing in my success had prepared me for the failure of stasis, of doing nothing. I was spoiled, used to people calling me for lunch. Now I had to call them. And when the phone rang and rang, or when I couldn't get through because of a protective secretary's old runaround, it really began to hurt. Furthermore, no one called me to ask me to go to work, which I figured would happen. What was I going to do for the rest of my life? The world had refuted the notion of a lifetime job, as it has for millions of others in the real world. But I was only thinking about myself. At the time, I was 51 and in relatively good health. I had years left—or did I? I felt I was a bit too old to start over, and a bit too young to quit working.

I couldn't go back to work at ESPN. I had learned, rather depressingly, that there was no urgency to return phone calls or to initiate any real business communication because I was out of the loop. Bill Grimes, who had replaced Chet Simmons, who left in 1982 to become commissioner of the USFL, was now reporting to ABC, an established television company, where the policies and procedures were certified and time-tested. He had moved up fast since he had been hired on in 1980 as a humble program coordinator. When ABC purchased ESPN from Texaco, and then Chief

Executive Officer Grimes left ESPN, Steve Bornstein was promoted as his replacement. Things turned from bad to worse for me. He could see where he was standing now and didn't have to deal with Getty Oil: he could shun its biggest symbol, yours truly.

I had written him, but Bornstein simply would not return my letters. One of those is what I call a come-to-Jesus letter. I wasn't asking for a lot. I said some of us old-timers would like to be remembered from time to time. We'd welcome the opportunity to come to anniversary parties. I reminded him that Simmons and I had made room for him and his success at ESPN. I liked Bornstein and I thought he had a good sense of humor. But unfortunately, he had a short memory when it came to recognizing the importance of the past and those who had given him the opportunity for the success he was enjoying. I think Bornstein's problem was his ego. I believe he was insecure and was trying to establish himself as a leader at ESPN, but my own ego suffered for it. Right then, at a very important transition point in my life, I needed to belong somewhere, and I couldn't even belong to a once-a-year party at ESPN. (By 2004, Bornstein was working for the NFL and negotiating a new billion-plus dollar package for the league with television.)

Over the years, I considered myself a controlled drinker, the man no one could tell was drinking. But I could tell. I wasn't a slob drunk. I just drank a lot of the time. In that age of business, businesspeople did that. There were often martinis at lunch and drinks after work. If we traveled, sleep wasn't an option until we put on a nightcap or two or three. Then sleep came more easily, we thought then.

I had a second residence in Palm Desert, a bright, two-story, brick home overlooking the golf course, which I had had for some time. I found myself spending more and more time there. I was still maintaining equilibrium, so to speak—not falling over drunk, but nonetheless drinking to my ailing heart's content. The occasional chest pains weren't going to scare me. I was tough and strong. When I ended up with a DUI to my name on the police records, that didn't bother me much either. It was the cost of being what I was. Anyway, I had gotten a ticket for drinking and driving before, and I had never changed my lifestyle as a result. I was beginning to feel like it was too late for meaningful change in my life.

I still thought of Daniels, and one day, I decided I needed to see about the Betty Ford Center, a prominent alcohol treatment place where many of the California glitterati have taken their pain and problems. When I went over the next day, I expected them to meet me with open arms, as if I was a prominent business leader who had the money. I was surprised to find the staff I met there very reserved. I knew nothing about all of this, nothing about Alcoholics Anonymous or anything. They asked me a range of questions, such as what I was doing for a living and where I lived. Basic questions.

"Can I come over tomorrow morning and enroll?" I asked.

There was a dulling silence.

"I don't have anything to do, I'm ready."

"Well, we'll let you know."

Was this some special club? It looked like it from the facilities and grounds. But I had belonged to plenty of exclusive clubs. I wondered, beginning to feel less special, whether I was a sufficiently bad case. Inside, I knew I was, whether I was in control or not. I was spiritually dead.

The nurse continued to scribble on the preapplication. Here I was with my best suit on, an expressed desire to change, money in my pocket, and they seemed to be looking at me and questioning whether or not they even wanted me. I was not accustomed to that kind of scrutiny.

"Can I come over tomorrow?" I asked again. "I don't have anything to do. I'm ready to—"

"We'll let you know."

"I have a friend here, Bill Daniels—if you'd like to talk to him."

The nurse smiled. "I'm sure he'd talk."

I sat around in the lobby watching people come in and go out, wondering whether their lives had mirrored mine. I waited and I waited there. The nurse finally told me a decision could not be made that day and that I should wait at home to be contacted. Perhaps it was her way of reminding me that I was a control freak. Well, so what! I knew that. The characteristic had served me well in business. But I had to start. I had to start now. I could give up being a control freak. Hell, I was out of control already, wasn't I? It was as if they had recognized in me that weakness and wanted to break me down. I wasn't in control. I couldn't be as long as I was alcohol dependent.

But I went home and I waited—eight days and counting. I'd have to wait just like the rest of them. The ninth day came and went like the others, and I felt like the smallest player in a group of boys waiting to be picked. I'd settle for last, just for the pickup game—if there were a pickup.

Then on the 10th day, I finally got the call. An admittance secretary said, "We'd like to have you come over on Thursday at 9:00." I was excited because I had been ready to give up and leave for what would have been a dangerous future, but now the Betty Ford Center was admitting me! Immediately, I dialed my wife, Shirley, and she brought my youngest daughter, Susan, down from Los Angeles.

That night, I was in a strange, almost eerie mood, wondering what I was getting myself into. I wondered whether I even needed to go—like the second thoughts I'd get before jumping into a business deal. I wasn't falling down drunk. I was providing for my family. If I wanted to go to Betty Ford, why would I second-guess myself? I couldn't sleep because I knew that I couldn't prepare for whatever was going to happen at the Center. I felt like I was going to a palace and didn't know the arcane greetings for the king and queen, or even where the rooms were and behind whose doors I could find the secrets. My method of operation had always been to try to know how to deal with the players and to know where the doors to everything led. I was going to be caught off guard in this new place. I would be laid bare, and it petrified me.

I went through evaluations at the Betty Ford Center and thought back to the requisite mental evaluation I had at Getty Oil in 1971, the actual text of which I discovered several years later. In the report, the psychologist, Clarence Genovese, Ph.D., said that I ranked high in decisiveness. Funny, but checking into the Betty Ford clinic I felt anything but decisive. Genovese went on to note the following: "In mental resources this individual is very intelligent, flexible, adaptable, and capable of doing overall thinking in a very high management position. Besides showing creative tendencies of his own, he is open-minded and receptive to the ideas of others." Over the years, I'd looked at the report several times—an ego grabber. But now, I didn't think I was smart or flexible or receptive—if I still had any of those characteristics. I felt like a person on the edge, controlled by something else, a failure on a one-way trip to someplace I couldn't know, but feared.

Like I said, my personality required me to be in control—always. I didn't like to look as though someone was giving me something new or that something was coming about which I knew nothing. For example, I didn't know what they did at a treatment facility. Would they give me a pill to get me to stop drinking? That's how naïve I was about it all.

And so that night, the night before admittance, when I couldn't undercut the tension with a good sleep, I decided I'd get up and have a cup of coffee and put in a little vodka. Then I tried lying on the couch, watching television, and trying to sleep. I would doze off and awaken, nervous. I'd have another modified coffee and pass into a weak sleep. Then I woke to the perfect test pattern on the screen and had another cup of what I thought would sustain me.

After I had breakfast, my wife drove me the two miles to the Betty Ford Center. I felt a bit meek and humbled when I spoke to the admittance nurse. I still felt uncomfortable when I saw two patients walk up, wide-eyed and smiling. They approached and grabbed my bags. "OK, you can go with these guys," the nurse said. We headed toward the residence hall. I felt apprehensive as hell, but I went with them, though I must admit, I thought of turning tail and running away. I still was in control, though, for no one seemed to know I was skittish and frightened to the core. Inside, I kept wondering what it would be like. Was I glad that I had come here? I kept thinking that this wasn't one of those desperate things that I had to do. No judge had ordered me into treatment. I could play the denial game so well. Mine wasn't the only case of denial. Sometime later, when my mother was asked where I was and what I was doing, she answered, "I think he's with President Ford. They're good friends. He meets with him every night these days."

Break-time coincided with my arrival at the residence hall. I steeled myself for the meeting. I'll forever remember this: it's what is called the "awakening." It all started when someone said, "Hey, guys, this is Stu." No sooner had the words passed along with the cigarette smoke from his mouth, than the rest of the men there got up and put their arms around me. And, mercy, I can't tell you how much I hated that. I was accustomed to building little barriers to keep others at a distance. I've read about intimate distances being between something like 18 inches and four feet. "Don't get too close, you might find out the real Stu."

I still felt superior. I wanted to be sure they knew who I was. But for some reason, I didn't say anything. I wanted to say, "Jeez, I've done a lot better things than you guys have. I started ESPN. You know ESPN. We have it here. I can turn it on for you."

But for a moment, it seemed the parade would never end. And then I went from feeling the unusual loneliness and isolation, even within the collective arms of the residence, to feeling new, changed—almost. It was that very last guy, a little, short guy, who happened to be from Denver—a city over which great satellites circled—who encircled me with his arms and then stood back with a puckish little smile. He said, "Damn, you smell good." It turned out he had used his sufficiently trained nose to sniff out the vodka on me from the night before.

It was like stepping into the dark and then immediately into the light. You think you've adjusted to the absence of light, and then it sears you. I felt like I was just stripped and undressed right there. I was embarrassed because he had caught me. And in the chess game of my life, I had no place to move. I had no alibi. I couldn't turn to him and say, "You must be smelling yourself." The son of a bitch had been in there for five weeks. As the rest of them laughed easily at the revelation—they had likely come in smelling of booze—I just kind of mumbled something.

I felt as foolish as J. Paul Getty must have felt when he took me once for a short ride. He had this 1969 Cadillac that he'd owned for some time, and as he drove me down about three blocks, it was clear from his look that he enjoyed driving it. He got out of the car—the doors were locked—and he came all the way around to my side of the car, a key prominent in his hand. As bright and obliging as a chauffeur, he unlocked the door. As he reached the other side and climbed back in slowly, I said, "Mr. Getty, do your automatic doors not work?" and I reached over and flicked them on and off. "See, you don't have to go around. You can flick this." He was stultified. He seemed to have no will to change.

I was riding alone now, then suddenly the obvious came to *me*, and I had an invitingly inexplicable feeling inside. It was an epiphany, and I quite simply knew it would be easy to quit. That was a one-shot kind of experience and by no means typical of alcoholics.

People can learn to have that feeling. But it hit me then—like an uppercut to the gut that lifts you off the ground—and, to this day, never have I had the occasion, in the 19 years since, to ever want to have a drink again. It was a bolt of lightning in my soul.

The people at the Betty Ford Center had let me cool my heels; my friend's hug had combined to restore my soul. I had 28 days there, which quietly passed, during which time I met several inmates I would count as friends, even though I would return to my home and perhaps never see them again. The men there didn't care who I was, nor did I care who they were. As far as ESPN went, I would sit in the lounge at Betty Ford Center and watch my old life switched as quickly as a channel, and though I followed ESPN as it moved into the broadcasting of major live sports, made changes, and grew to include Major League Baseball, the National Football League, and the National Basketball Association, and I didn't need to talk about it. It was more like "been-there, done-that."

On Sunday, we could have guests, and I still learn from the full love that my daughters began to show me. They brought cookies, and we sat out on the green next to some movie star who drank artificial wine with his girlfriend, as if the wine were real, as if the blanket could take them magically elsewhere. Perhaps it did.

In my old life, I had handled a $10 million checking account, which felt like my own, and now I looked in dismay at my own checkbook. I had a large settlement package from Getty when the company was sold, but not large by today's standards. No one had employment contracts. Throw in divorce settlements and income tax, then I had some big dents in my bank account, and I knew my future was less than assured.

EPILOGUE

As I look back, I realize I've been blessed with so many varied opportunities, some of which I have described in this book. I've been at the right place at the right time (that's luck), and have been fortunate enough to seize the moment (that's life).

Today, I am an admiring fan, though no longer officially associated with ESPN. I can never escape those nostalgic reveries whenever I watch the great sports network. They sometimes overwhelm me so that I lose my fix on the action. I am amazed and proud when I consider the phenomenal growth of this enterprise in the short span of 25 years. When I see images of the sprawling broadcast center in Bristol, Connecticut, with its myriad satellite Earth stations pointing to the sky, I'm reminded of the day when the first show was broadcast from a mobile television truck, hastily modified and equipped, when construction of the broadcast building failed to meet launch deadline.

In those days, most of the staff and visitors stayed at a small local motel in Bristol, the Farmington Inn. Today, two major hotel chains are represented on or near the ESPN campus. In those halcyon days, too, most employees shared large rented homes and "hot-bedded"—the term used for those who worked 12-hour shifts and shared bedrooms: thus, the bed was always warm.

Today, hundreds of ESPN families call Bristol and its surrounding communities their home. The children they are raising can never recall the ESPN of one building, three satellite Earth stations, and an unpaved parking lot. Oh yes! Those were the days—as were all the days, weeks, and months in those giddy beginning years. Those who initially began watching ESPN—and no one really knew just how many did—were introduced to sporting events never before seen on television: kick-box karate, Australian-rules football, college lacrosse, and slow-pitch softball, to name but a few. Much of these owe their coverage simply to economic exigencies, for both capital and the availability of other more traditional events were scarce. Fortunately, sports lovers persisted, and gradually, as the flow of advertising dollars grew and cable operators began to pay subscriber fees, ESPN found the capital clout it needed to acquire rights for broadcasting major live events.

Those early years yielded some very good times. Often, at private parties or at Getty Oil Company social gatherings, I was asked to find out the game score for someone's favorite school. I could pick up the phone, speak with someone at the broadcast center, and, much to my delight, the on-air announcer would immediately meet the request. An ego trip, perhaps, but when the chairman of the board, Harold Berg, or another important Getty executive—or some skeptical friends—were asking the favor, I was only too willing to give it. And so be it. The more I could do to keep people interested and connected with ESPN, the smoother became the ongoing selling job to keep the network alive.

I found that having one of the Getty corporate jets available to attend major sporting events was a fine perk. We often hosted advertising clients and sports personalities at the NCAA Final Four basketball championship, the World Series, the Super Bowl, the Davis Cup tennis tournament in the United States and Europe, and major golf tournaments.

On one of these occasions, I invited the ABC television crew to join me on our plane for the British Open in Scotland. It was the first time

ESPN was televising the Thursday–Friday rounds. Bob Rosberg, Jack Whitaker, and the late Dave Marr were needling me about the insignificance of ESPN compared to ABC, at the time, a rather facile argument much like comparing a minnow to a whale. While I couldn't deny it, I came back, tongue in cheek, with the only response I felt appropriate: "Wait and see, guys. One day you'll be working for ESPN." And not too long after ABC purchased controlling interest in ESPN, sports announcers began to wear two hats—not exactly what I had in mind when I made the comment on the airplane, but I was somehow able to make good on what must have seemed to them an extravagant boast.

Recently, ESPN has established itself as the most dominant brand for Disney, the current owner, and is one of the most recognized names in sports with its seven domestic networks, magazine, restaurants, and forays into radio and interactive computer games. According to Kagan Research, ESPN had the most revenue in 2003 among the top networks and was the second most profitable. I believe those lofty achievements can be attributed to the fortuitous succession of ownership that began when the vision of ESPN was realized: Getty Oil Company took the risk when all other options proved fickle or simply declined; ABC brought to the company a powerful infusion of broadcast talent and management; Capital Cities introduced sound fiscal responsibility; and Disney, with its sports franchises and sound cross promotions, has imparted to ESPN an enhanced *E* for entertainment.

In recent years, as I have traveled around the country speaking at colleges and universities, I have drawn from the brothers of my college fraternity, Phi Gamma Delta, the inspiration I needed to chronicle my ESPN memories. They must be the single most enthusiastic group of sports junkies anywhere, with their television sets tuned to *SportsCenter* around the clock.

Don Rasmussen, a key employee of ESP-TV in the short, pre-Evey days, supports the contention that I am the founder of what certainly has become a preeminent network. I take great pride in being part of the founding of ESPN. That role has afforded me the opportunity to meet many of the top sports personalities and to attend major sporting events throughout the world.

As Don King would say, "Only in America."